Praise for *Psalms*

"Reading meditatively, *Psalms for Jesus* takes one into another stratosphere on many levels. Intellectually, it demands focus, calling one to a deeper level of thought. Spiritually, one is transported by the sheer overabundant love Jesus has for humans. Emotionally, one becomes caught in the self-surprising love for Jesus that has been hidden with works. In reading Dr. George Bebawi's writing, my striving turned to resting in love. This book has been written for these times, for all people."

—Jo Anne Lyon, Ambassador
General Superintendent Emerita
The Wesleyan Church

"George, a dear friend for a good thirty years, is one of the deepest theologians and best miners of Patristic jewels. He is a spiritual scholar that God has gifted to the Church, as you will discover when assimilating *Psalms for Jesus.* New generations of Christians are keenly seeking and reviving the Church by bringing to life and spreading George's experience of God's Love.

I will eternally be indebted to George for helping me discover the oceanic love of God and the genuine reality of His loving nature by introducing me to studying the Patristic Tradition. These Patristic Teachings inspired my heart and obliged my mind to write my two books in Arabic."

—Hany Mina Mikhail,
Consultant in Orthopaedic Surgery and
Emergency Medicine, UK (retired), and author of
Divine Justice is Life not Death, Forgiveness not Punishment
and *God, Man and the Universe*

"This is George Bebawi at his finest! With Israel's Old Covenant songbook in one hand and the New Covenant Incarnation of Christ in the other, a most beautiful collaboration is forged. These prayers have the potential to make you more fully human by purging the sanctimonious nature of much of our spirituality. Prepare for your soul to be exposed to the unbounded divine love of the Trinity!"

—Shane Fuller,
Pastor of The Dwelling Place

"When we hear the word Theology, most of us immediately have a mental image of scholarship, learnedness, arguments carefully reasoned out, and written in debate, in prose. Early theology was not so: it was prophetic, uttered in poetics, with imagery, metaphor, and vision, and theology's highest manifestation was in poems, with their capacity to enter deeply into mystery, to envision in language the longing for God that only the heart could know and no logic of argument could fully grasp. It is no accident that the Psalms became predominant texts for use in liturgical prayer. In the early church this appreciation of prayer-in-poetry was picked up especially in the East by writers such as Ephrem the Syrian and others, and continued as a major source of theologizing even when more formal reasoning, scholar's theology, came to dominate.

In *Psalms for Jesus*, George Bebawi has returned to the ancient tradition, producing a testimony to his faith in heart-felt utterances, a homage to the Biblical Psalms, which is deeply moving, powerfully prayerful. And yet Dr. Bebawi, an academic theologian of repute, has combined the poetics of the Psalms with his thorough understanding of doctrinal theology; his Psalms are prose poems, and into the imagery and the feeling he has woven a full body of theological ideas, and the result is a Christology which calls for a response of the whole soul, mind, and heart together."

—Prof. Richard Schneider,
co-Director, School of Orthodox Theology
at Trinity College, University of Toronto

"My endorsement of Dr. George Bebawi's book does not come from a scholarly background. Rather from a pilgrim who has been on the journey now for almost 75 years. It was because of my friendship with George while serving as a missionary in the Middle East that I was introduced to the writings and lives of the mystics of the past. For more than 50 years my soul has feasted upon the meditative life.

Now finally, the spiritual wisdom and insights that have been given to George by God's Holy Spirit are presented in a written form, translated from his Arabic version to English.

I commend, challenge, and encourage every true seeker after truth and an understanding of 'the breadth, length, height, and depth [of Christ's love]' to read these psalms with a prayerful heart. I'm sure that as I have experienced times of weeping as I began to understand more fully that everlasting eternal love and the connection between the divine and the human, you will also."

—Bob Hoskins,
Founder of OneHope

Psalms

for

JESUS

A Heart Longing for Union with Christ

Dedicated to my wife, May Rifka Bebawi,
the best human being I ever have known

Dr. George Bebawi
Author of *The Crown of Life: An Orthodox Perspective*

Psalms *for* JESUS

A Heart Longing for Union with Christ

Foreword by Dr. Sebastian Brock
Author of *The Syriac Fathers on Prayer and the Spiritual Life*

Cover photo, *Peaceful East Iceland*, by Markus Trienke taken at Sudur-Mulasysla, Iceland

Transcribed, organized, edited, and promoted by Emily Bopp, without whom this collection would have remained hidden.

Published in Indianapolis, Indiana by Epiphany Publishing, LLC.

For information about discounts available for bulk purchases, sales promotions, fund-raising, and educational needs, contact the Epiphany Publishing Sales Team at sales@epiphanypublishing.us.

Library of Congress Control Number: 2020931479

ISBN 9781946093141 (paperback)
ISBN 9781946093158 (eBook)

This book was printed in the United States of America.

E✦P

Epiphany Publishing
P.O. Box 36814
Indianapolis, IN 46236
www.epiphanypublishing.us
info@epiphanypublishing.us

Contents

Foreword xix

Psalm 1: Jesus – Our Epiphany of Divine Love 25
Psalm 2: A Lamentation of the Blindness of Human Power 26
Psalm 3: Jesus is My Peace 28
Psalm 4: Jesus – Our Inseparable Peace 29
Psalm 5: Jesus – Pleasure and Freedom 30
Psalm 6: Jesus – Gentle Healer 31
Psalm 7: Jesus – Our Song of Salvation 32
Psalm 8: Jesus, Your Name is the Glory of Humanity 33
Psalm 9: Jesus Caught Me, to My Great Delight 34
Psalm 10: Jesus' Bitter Labor Yields Glorious Fruit 36
Psalm 11: Jesus – Lover of Mankind Calling Us to Our Senses 38
Psalm 12: Jesus Put to Death the Condemnation of Death 40
Psalm 13: Singing Jesus' Solidarity with Us 42
Psalm 14: Jesus – the Authentication of Our Humanity 43
Psalm 15: Jesus' Glory of Self-Giving 44
Psalm 16: Jesus – Our Eternal and Everlasting Inheritance 45
Psalm 17: Jesus – Our Glimpse of Fiery Love 47
Psalm 18: Jesus – the Pleasure of Serving 48
Psalm 19: Jesus – Giver of Life in Spite of Illness and Death 49
Psalm 20: Jesus – Our Sweet Communion 50
Psalm 21: Jesus' Overwhelming Gift of Love 51
Psalm 22: Jesus Judges Death to Give Us Life 52
Psalm 23: Jesus – the Good Shepherd 53
Psalm 24: Jesus – the Creator Who Became Human 54
Psalm 25: Jesus – Our Shared Immortality 55
Psalm 26: Jesus – the Divine Plan of Our Perfection 56
Psalm 27: Jesus – Gift of New Eternal Delight 57
Psalm 28: Jesus is the Covenant of Eternal Inheritance 58

Psalm 29: Song of the Transformation of our Humanity 59
Psalm 30: Jesus – Lover of Man 60
Psalm 31: Jesus – Our Eternal Anointing and Eternal Dwelling 61
Psalm 32: Jesus, Unhindered in His Love 62
Psalm 33: Jesus – the Freedom of Slaves 64
Psalm 34: Jesus is Our Assurance 65
Psalm 35: Jesus – Revealer and Giver of the Father's Mercy 66
Psalm 36: Jesus' Name Is the Divine Plan 67
Psalm 37: Jesus is the Revelation of Triune Love 68
Psalm 38: Jesus' Love Redefines Judgment 70
Psalm 39: Jesus Became Mortal for Our Sake 72
Psalm 40: Jesus is Our Savior, Divine and Human 74
Psalm 41: Jesus – Our Hymn of New Life 76
Psalm 42: Jesus – Song of Shared Love 78
Psalm 43: Jesus – the Judge of Death 80
Psalm 44: Jesus Shares Our Human Body 81
Psalm 45: The Taste of Your Love, Jesus, is Like Fire in my Heart. 82
Psalm 46: Jesus – Song of Hope and Firm Assurance 83
Psalm 47: Jesus is Our Root of Eternal Life 84
Psalm 48: Jesus – Our Sanctuary 85
Psalm 49: Jesus without Our Definitions 86
Psalm 50: Jesus – Song of Mercy and Forgiveness 88
Psalm 51: Jesus, Your Name is the Song of Love 89
Psalm 52: Jesus is the Flood of the Father's Love 90
Psalm 53: Jesus, Your Cross Is a Sign of Life 92
Psalm 54: Jesus – Our Cup of Love 93
Psalm 55: Jesus is Our Love and Our Life 95
Psalm 56: Jesus, with You There is No Guilt or Shame 96
Psalm 57: Jesus, into Your Hands We Deliver Our Life 98
Psalm 58: Jesus – the Light of Our Darkness 99
Psalm 59: Jesus – the Light of Every Generation 100
Psalm 60: Jesus – Unique Love 101
Psalm 61: Jesus – Giver of Life 102
Psalm 62: Jesus – the Healer of Our Distorted Vision 103
Psalm 63: Jesus – Our Spring of Life 105
Psalm 64: Jesus – Our Fountain of Eternal Life 106
Psalm 65: Jesus – Conqueror of Death 107
Psalm 66: Jesus Changes Our Mortal Life to Heavenly Life 109

Psalm 67: Jesus – Purity of the Impure 110
Psalm 68: Jesus Clothed Our Nakedness with Dignity 112
Psalm 69: Jesus – Union of God and Humanity 113
Psalm 70: Jesus Revealed Divine Love, Beyond Definition 115
Psalm 71: Jesus, Discovered by Love 117
Psalm 72: Jesus, Unfading Light and Life 118
Psalm 73: Jesus – in Us to Grow and to Mature 119
Psalm 74: Jesus is the End of Fear and Death 120
Psalm 75: Jesus is Eternally Divine and Human for Humanity 121
Psalm 76: Jesus is Born Every Moment into Human Filth 122
Psalm 77: Jesus is Revealed to Share His Life 123
Psalm 78: Jesus – Our Purification and Freedom 124
Psalm 79: Jesus Unmasked Our Humanity 125
Psalm 80: A Psalm for Jesus, My Brother 127
Psalm 81: Jesus – Our True Union with the Father 128
Psalm 82: Jesus – the Deification of Love 130
Psalm 83: Jesus – Our Dwelling in the Love of the Father 132
Psalm 84: Jesus – Our Prayer to the Father in the Holy Spirit 133
Psalm 85: Jesus, Our Hearts Are Your Favorite Dwelling Place 136
Psalm 86: Jesus is Our Eternal Bond 137
Psalm 87: Jesus – the Hope of the Fallen 139
Psalm 88: Jesus is Our Glory 140
Psalm 89: Jesus – Confirmation of the Covenant of Divine Love 142
Psalm 90: Jesus – the Fire of the Eternal Flame of Love 143
Psalm 91: Jesus – the Dwelling of the Triune Love 144
Psalm 92: Jesus – Divine Touch of Life and Hope 145
Psalm 93: Jesus – Breath of Love 146
Psalm 94: Jesus – a Song for the Lover of My Soul 147
Psalm 95: Jesus – Immortal Joy of Our Humanity 149
Psalm 96:
- I - Jesus Crucified and Risen for Us 151
- II - The Divine Triumph 152
- III - Your Cross is Your Kiss for Sinners 152
- IV - Your Love is My Meditation 153
- V - Your Love is Wonderful 153
- VI - Freedom from Sin, Condemnation and Hell 154
- VII - You Alone Are My Life 154
- VIII - Your Love is Freedom 155

IX - Your Name Unites Me to You 156
X - Bridegroom of My Soul 156
XI - How Can I Love like You? 156
XII - Your Cross is Most Dear to Me 157
XIII - Jesus My Good Shepherd 157
XIV - Your Patient Love Guides Me 158
XV - Your Cross and Your Resurrection Are Your Victory 159
XVI - Your Cross is Special Wisdom 159
XVII - Your Call is Always Sweet 160
Psalm 97:
I - Your Cross is a Lantern to My Life 161
II - Your Cross Put an End to My Old Way of Life 161
III - I Can Not Love You by My Strength Alone 162
IV - Your Love Has its Law; to Give to the Unworthy 162
V - My Love is Weak 163
VI - No Limits for Your Love 164
VII - You Save Us by Faith, Not by Knowledge 165
VIII - Give Me a Share in Your Love 165
Psalm 98: Jesus is the Wounded Love 167
Psalm 99: Jesus – Our Crucified, Risen Shepherd 168
Psalm 100: Jesus – the Hand of Peace 169
Psalm 101: Jesus – Tender Caring Wisdom 170
Psalm 102: Jesus is My Dwelling Place 171
Psalm 103: Jesus Can Not Be Divided 172
Psalm 104: Jesus, Our Creator, Transforms Death into Life 173
Psalm 105: Jesus – Love, Life, and Freedom in One 174
Psalm 106: Jesus – the Beauty of Divine Love 175
Psalm 107: Jesus – Endless Self-Giving 176
Psalm 108: Jesus – Our Savior Before the Creation of the Cosmos 178
Psalm 109: Jesus, Your Kenosis Continues 179
Psalm 110: Jesus Has No Room for Ethnicity 182
Psalm 111: Jesus – Purity in our Filth 183
Psalm 112: Jesus – Compassion above Human Judgment 184
Psalm 113: Jesus Judges with Love 186
Psalm 114: Jesus Speaks through the Holy Spirit 187
Psalm 115: Jesus Unites Us by His Love, Not Our Achievement.. 188
Psalm 116: Jesus, in You Words and Actions Are the Same 189

Psalm 117: Jesus, Your Birth Has Honored Women 190
Psalm 118: Jesus is Our Freedom from the Chains of the Law 191
Psalm 119: Jesus' Love Has No Equal 192
Psalm 120: Jesus Did Not Live for Himself 193
Psalm 121: Jesus Inspires Maturity 195
Psalm 122: Jesus - the Altar Where We Meet................................. 196
Psalm 123: Jesus - Supper of Love.. 197
Psalm 124: Jesus is a Healing Justice 198
Psalm 125: Jesus, in You We Discovered Our Humanity 199
Psalm 126: Jesus, in You God Honored Us...................................... 200
Psalm 127: Jesus, in You We Discover God 201
Psalm 128: Jesus, Your Heart is Our Room in the Divine 203
Psalm 129: Jesus, Your Path is Life 204
Psalm 130: Jesus, Our Words Failed to Contain You 206
Psalm 131: Jesus - Gift of Life Manifested in and Outside Time .. 207
Psalm 132: Jesus is God's Way to Us 208
Psalm 133: Jesus Releases Time from the Clutch of Death............ 209
Psalm 134: Jesus - the Foundation of Our Union 210
Psalm 135: Jesus, You Came to Share Your Being with Us 211
Psalm 136: Jesus is Divinity Shining in Poor and Sick Humanity. 213
Psalm 137: Jesus - Love Given to the Unworthy 214
Psalm 138: Jesus Receives the Anointing of the Spirit of the Father's Love.. 215
Psalm 139: Jesus Gives without Asking for a Response 217
Psalm 140: Jesus, in You Love Became Participation 218
Psalm 141: Jesus is Heavenly Life Grafted in Our Earthly Life 219
Psalm 142: Jesus' Words and Actions Revealed One Life 220
Psalm 143: Jesus is the Guarantee of the Communion of Love 221
Psalm 144: Jesus' Being is Truth, Not Ideas..................................... 222
Psalm 145: Jesus, Sharing Your Life is Your Goal 223
Psalm 146: Jesus' Heart Beats with Ours 224
Psalm 147: Jesus is Our True Life... 225
Psalm 148: Jesus is Our Human Body in the Godhead.................. 226
Psalm 149: Jesus - Our Human Awareness...................................... 228
Psalm 150: Jesus - Our Freedom 229
Psalm 151: In Jesus, Humanity is the Crown of Heaven and Earth 230
Psalm 152: Jesus, Loving You is Freedom 232

Psalm 153: Jesus is the Seal of Unbroken Divine-Human Love 234
Psalm 154: Jesus is the Human Who Did Not Live for Himself.... 236
Psalm 155: Jesus – Your Delight in Being with Us 238
Psalm 156: Jesus, There is No Punishment in You 241
Psalm 157: Jesus, the Married and the Celibate Are Your Inheritance 243
Psalm 158: Jesus' Name is More Precious Than the Whole Earth. 245
Psalm 159: Jesus – A Lament for Misunderstanding Your Presence.. 246
Psalm 160: Jesus Gives a New Name 248
Psalm 161: Jesus is the Love above Academic Christology 250
Psalm 162: Jesus, No One is like You 252
Psalm 163: Jesus is Our Sabbath of Rest... 253
Psalm 164: Jesus – the New Boundaries of Our New Creation..... 254
Psalm 165: Jesus – Forgiveness is Your Nature 257
Psalm 166: Jesus – True Love that Unites 258
Psalm 167: Jesus – Our Freedom from Condemnation.................. 260
Psalm 168: Jesus – the Beginning and the End............................... 261
Psalm 169: Jesus, Your Incarnation Was Not Words or Debates .. 262
Psalm 170: Jesus, Your Incarnation is Beyond Our Use of Words 264
Psalm 171: Jesus, the Second Adam 266
Psalm 172: Jesus – in Worship, We Become Persons 267
Psalm 173: Jesus is Our Journey with God 268
Psalm 174: Jesus – Our Progress from Birth to Resurrection......... 271
Psalm 175: Jesus, You Made Us Your Divine Image....................... 272
Psalm 176: Jesus – Eternal Self-Emptying.. 273
Psalm 177: Jesus, in You Division Became Distinction.................. 274
Psalm 178: Jesus – Love and Self-Giving Revealed in Created Flesh 275
Psalm 179: Jesus, You Choose Our Flesh and Blood to Reveal Yourself.. 277
Psalm 180: Jesus, Your Humanity is What We Need to Read 278
Psalm 181: Jesus – Our Humanity Is at the Center of Revelation . 280
Psalm 182: Jesus, Your Name Encompasses Our Being 282
Psalm 183: Jesus Avoided Self-Defense 283
Psalm 184: Jesus – Fire of Divinity within Flesh and Blood........... 285
Psalm 185: Jesus – Circle of the Communion of Love 287
Psalm 186: Jesus, Your Love Made You Ignorant 289

Psalm 187: Jesus, the Sign of the Cross Is Your Seal 291
Psalm 188: Jesus, Our Hearts Are Your Resting Place 292
Psalm 189: Jesus - Divine Love Revealed in Silence 293
Psalm 190: Jesus, Unfamiliar Light 294
Psalm 191: Jesus - the Unspeakable Depth of Self-Giving 296
Psalm 192: Jesus - Our Covenant with God 298
Psalm 193: Jesus, Your Love is Unfamiliar 300
Psalm 194: Jesus, You Have Changed My Self-Knowledge 301
Psalm 195: Jesus - the Old Came to an End 302
Psalm 196: Jesus, in You There Is No Higher or Lower in the Bond of Divine Adoration 303
Psalm 197: Jesus Is Our Courage in Time of Death 304
Psalm 198: Jesus Came to Lift Us up to Divine Communion 306
Psalm 199: Jesus - Our New Freedom 307
Psalm 200: Jesus - the Past, the Present, and the Future 308

About the Author 311
About the Publisher 313

Foreword

It is only on extremely rare occasions that one is sent a text to read which leaves one deeply moved by the profundity of feeling expressed in it. This was very much the case when I received from George Bebawi, a Coptic Egyptian friend, the typescript of *Psalms for Jesus*: as my wife Helen and I read them, it quickly became obvious to us that these psalms were written from the heart and spoke to us in a way that was both direct and moving. The author, who happens also to be a friend of nearly fifty years standing from whom I have learnt much more than he is aware of, is a theologian who has suffered much, not least from misunderstanding by the authorities of his own Church. Deeply grounded in the writings of the Fathers, a number of which he has translated into Arabic, he is very much the sort of theologian who corresponds to Evagrius' famous saying 'If you are a theologian, you will pray in truth; if you pray in truth, you will be a theologian'. He adopts the genre of meditative and discursive prayers that are to be found in both Eastern and Western Christian traditions; one thinks especially of the beautiful Syriac Odes of Solomon from early Christianity, or the deeply-felt prayers by the medieval Armenian writer, St Gregory of Narek, or, in English, of the Centuries of Meditations by Thomas Traherne.

Running through these 200 psalms there are a number of prominent themes, the three most important of which might be singled out here: first the infinite nature of the divine love that lies behind the Incarnation and the sacrifice of the Cross; then, the humanity of Jesus as a sharing and state of being which is united with our humanity; and third, how, by responding to, and reciprocating with, this love that lies behind the Incarnation, we discover not only what it means to have Jesus as our brother with whom we are united, but also that we human beings thereby have the potential of becoming 'partakers of the divine nature' (2 Peter 1:4). Underlying all this is the idea that the purpose of the Incarnation is to effect an exchange which St Athanasius and St Ephrem (who both happened to die in the same year, 373) expressed in similar ways:

> God became a human being so that a human being might become god (Athanasius);

and

> He gave us divinity, we gave him humanity (Ephrem).

Love as the prime motivation for the Incarnation and for the sacrifice of the Cross is an emphasis found notably in the writings of another great Syriac author, Isaac of Nineveh, who wrote:

> The entire purpose of our Lord's death was not to redeem us from sins, or for any other reason, but solely in order that the world might become aware of the love which God has for creation. Had all this astounding affair taken place solely for the purpose of the forgiveness of sin, it would have been sufficient to redeem us by some other means.

This emphasis on the primacy of divine love, and its supreme manifestation in the Cross, is recurrent in *Psalms for Jesus*: thus, for example:

> Your Incarnation testifies to your love for humanity,
> Your cross is the crown of your love (no. 19).

> I meditate on your cross. When I begin to look for a reason for your love, I stumble; but the path of your love is far above our understanding (no. 96, section 2).

Nos. 96 and 97, each with a number of sections, are essentially meditations on the connections between the Cross and love. The effect of the realization of this divine love is dramatic:

> I will make the sign of the cross

It is like the knife of your love.
It cuts off all the values that have been established in our world,
Those that have shamed the life I have lived without you (no. 77).

The second of the central themes mentioned above happens to have been well brought out by some of the phraseology to be found in the writings of the early Syriac Fathers, who frequently employed the everyday imagery of putting on, and taking off, clothing as a metaphor to describe the different stages of salvation history; thus one of the ways by which they expressed the mystery of the Incarnation was to say that God the Word 'put on our humanity', or even 'He put on us', thus bringing out how the union of the divinity and humanity in the incarnate Christ is also the union of His humanity with our humanity.

This closeness between the humanity of Jesus and our humanity can be upsetting to our normal way of thinking, as is brought out in the following:

O my Love, your love is both divine and human
But is one Love of the one Lord and the one Savior.
We are afraid of the divine but we are also afraid of the human
And therefore, union is a problem for us.
Union is what we cannot accept, but division is what we love.
We find our ego in our divisions and we love them
Because we are afraid to give up what we like and what we love.
True deification is the fruit of your love.
We cannot achieve it or have it from any other source,
Only from your union with us (no. 82).

But once the implications are accepted, then it is possible to exclaim:

Blessed are you, Lord,
Who unified my being with yours when you became human.
What a great mystery is your incarnate love (no. 137).

Such a sense of unity with Christ was expressed long ago by St Gregory of Nazianzus, the Theologian par excellence, in a dramatic way in one of his Orations:

> Yesterday I was crucified with Christ,
> Today I am glorified with Him;
> Yesterday I died with Him,
> Today I am made alive with Him;
> Yesterday I was buried with Him,
> Today I rise with him.
> Let us make an offering to the One who died and rose again for us,
> … Let us offer our own selves ... the possession most precious to God and closest to Him;
> Let us give back to the Image that which is according to the Image, recognizing our own value,
> Honoring the Archetype, knowing the power of the Mystery and for whom Christ died.

In the realization of the potential implied by the humanity of Christ being our humanity, it is love, not knowledge, which needs to be the starting point for any further understanding. That knowledge of the divine world is dependent on love, and not on human knowledge, is expressed on several occasions:

> For you, Lord, love comes before knowledge;
> For us, knowledge comes before everything (no. 186).

> It is only by participation in the communion of love
> That we can receive knowledge –
> Pure knowledge that has no earthly goals.
> O Teacher of Love, you love us without reason,
> But for a good purpose:
> To give us a share in your eternal life (no. 140).

Divine love does not impose itself, but awaits in patience for a response:

> You are hidden and tucked away within the creases of my being
> So as not to obstruct my freedom…

For you are not shy to call us your brother,
But the shyness of your love compels you not to interfere.
That is why you stand knocking at the door
Waiting for us to open the door of our perception (no. 71).

When the response of love comes, it needs to reflect the way in which the divine love is initially offered:

O Lover of Man,
Those who love with your humbleness and
Take your humbleness to the depth of their life,
They will discover in those depths your pleasure in them (no. 5).

The divine offer of love is completely free, and there is never any question of worthiness:

In every talk about worthiness,
There is a black cloud that tries to hide the light of your love (no. 137).

The Sacraments play an important role, providing paradigms of the intended union between the humanity of Jesus and that of individual Christians, as is made clear in a number of places (notably nos. 15, 21, 42, and 48); at the same time these same Sacraments are subject to misunderstanding and abuse (nos. 145, 159; similarly, on Christmas, no.76). Such misunderstanding is often due to allocating to knowledge a priority over love:

We have accumulated too many volumes on the two natures [in Christ],
But there is not one single volume on the
One divine incarnate love...
We like to divide the divine and the human because that suits us
Because the union of love is utterly unfamiliar to us (no. 161).

and

In deep pain, I cry to you, Spring of Life.

We have learned from theology that you are distinct from us,
But our theology never taught us the mystery of your
Union with us.
When I remember your Incarnation, my soul weeps.
I need that same union of your divinity and your humanity,
To be anointed by the Father with you,
To become a christ.
My deep longing is to be one with you (no. 147).

Not surprisingly, resort is made to the language and the imagery of the Song of Songs when describing the intensity and intimacy of any encounter with divine love:

The taste of Your love, Jesus, is like fire in my heart (no. 45).

Jesus, come and give a kiss.
His kiss is a word.
His word is his lips.
His lips are his promise.
His promise is his person (no. 94).

Lord Jesus,
You are in me
And I am in you,
Forever (no. 4).

Throughout *Psalms for Jesus* the images and concepts are deeply grounded in the biblical writings and those of the Church Fathers, but at the same time the way in which ideas are expressed is both fresh and contemporary. They offer a truly wonderful resource.

Dr. Sebastian Brock
Emeritus Reader in Syriac Studies,
Oxford University
and Fellow of the British Academy

Psalm 1

Jesus – Our Epiphany of Divine Love

Blessed are you Lord Jesus.
By your incarnation you have revealed to us the way of life,
By your cross you have shown us the ugly face of evil.
Your cross is the triumph of forgiveness.
You have illumined our life by your life and by your teaching.
This way of life does not lead to sin and death.
You have granted us a communion with your saints.
Communion and illumination are the delight
Of those who seek to take up your way.

Blessed are you Lord Jesus.
The law of your cross is the strength of our love,
The power of your resurrection is my refuge from the fear of death.
Your cross and your resurrection are my strength day and night.
You have grafted us into your holy body
And into the life of your Father,
You have made us a new creation, free from condemnation,
Bringing fruit to the vine of your kingdom, your holy church.

As for the way of unfaithfulness,
It is like dust that has no stability, the winds of doubt
Can take it anywhere.
But you, Lord Jesus, have given us the stability of your eternal life.
We will not perish by the death of sin.
Glory be to you,
Lover of Humanity.

Psalm 2

A Lamentation of the Blindness of Human Power

Why do the nations despise your incarnation
And your inexpressible humility that made you become human?
Vain is their glory that seeks to crush human life,
For those who renounce your cross have fallen into the trap
Of the love of power where there is no mercy in their hearts.
They love destruction
Those who despise your cross and blaspheme your love.
Truly they are themselves enchained with the chain of slavery,
Living in the pit of hatred.

As for those who ask, "Why have you been crucified?"
They do not know that the sickness of sin is in the heart.
They do not know that your life-giving death
Has penetrated our being,
Has uprooted the roots of evil in us.

As for us,
According to your call,
We carry our cross every day
Because it is by the cross
That we shall trample all the unholy desires of the soul.

You have anointed us and made us eternal children
In your eternal, heavenly kingdom,
This is why the world does not understand, but fights us
And brutally opposes us.

But you, Lord Jesus,
Crucified and risen from the dead,
You have defeated power by humility.
You have dispersed hatred by mercy.

So it is that those who have hardness of heart

Cannot stand in your presence.
But you, Lord, can overcome all weakness, even hardness of heart,
For nothing can halt your mercy.
Blessed are those who trust in your mercy,
For your mercy is always new every day.

Psalm 3

Jesus is My Peace

Lord Jesus,
How many are the thoughts that disturb me?
Like the numberless waves of the sea,
They crash over my head and steal my breath.
But you are the Savior who is mighty,
Who can silence any storm in the heart of man.
Your peace mutes our violent ideas.
Say the word, Lord Jesus, and the warmth of the sun
Will break through these clouds.

You are my salvation, Lord Jesus,
My Lord in whom I trust.
Your cross is my shield,
Your resurrection is the glory of my eternal life.

You do not forget those who have been united with you
At your holy altar.
Your salvation is like a flood of rivers,
Which can topple every obstacle.

Salvation is from you,
Lord Jesus,
Only by the power of your cross and resurrection
We shall overcome.

Psalm 4

Jesus – Our Inseparable Peace

When I call you, you hear me,
Because you are one with me and with us,
The first-born among many brothers and sisters.
Tribulations cannot separate us,
They pass very quickly.
You alone are the true Savior.
There is no salvation from humans.
How could a mortal save another mortal?

When I see my weakness and my deficiency,
How they fight me.
I cry out to you, my strength,
That I may sacrifice every hidden desire, to remain one with you
As a holy living sacrifice.

Lord Jesus, you alone are my joy.
What humans can offer may help for a time, but will perish.
Yet he who is filled with your pleasure and divine joy
Cannot seek anything else,
For you are the tranquility of the soul.

In my loneliness,
You are with me.
You seek those who are alone,
You have taken their solitude in you
That they may seek your face.

Lord Jesus,
You are in me
And I am in you,
Forever.

Psalm 5

Jesus – Pleasure and Freedom

When the light of the day breaks into the darkness,
It is like the light of your resurrection that has enlightened our life.
You have given us life, Lord Jesus.
Your joy is in hearing our prayers.
The glory that we offer to you
Pleases your heart.

O Lover of Man,
Those who love with your humbleness
And take your humbleness to the depth of their life,
They will discover in those depths, your pleasure in them.
They will become an icon of your self-emptying,
Of your coming down from heaven for us,
And so, they are saved from narcissism.

In the sanctuaries of our churches, the places
You have chosen to reveal your grace,
We come.
You have called us to stand in front of your holy altar
So we kneel down to your great love.
In our kneeling, we re-discover your incarnation
And your true self-surrender.
Because by your self-surrender, even to the cross,
You have sown the seed of the resurrection in your body
As a pledge for our coming resurrection.
By your resurrection, you have grafted us
Into the life of your good Father,
To make us heirs of your kingdom,
By the power of the Holy Spirit.

Glory be to you,
Lover of Man.

Psalm 6

Jesus – Gentle Healer

Lord Jesus Christ
Your love chastises me,
Your compassion straightens the hidden thoughts of my heart,
Your humility judges me and teaches me mercy.

In love you are weak, and come down from glory.
You heal my fear of judgment which was planted by my guilt.
You judged judgment itself by your cross.
Abolished death,
Destroyed corruption.
Yes, your mercy is the secret joy of my soul,
For you have saved me from death.
The chain of sin has been broken.
The verdict of death has been removed forever.

In the garden, you prayed and wept and asked
For the release of life from the fear of death.

When I forget you for a while, I long to return to you.
My tears comfort my soul.
The seed of love you placed in my heart cannot die.

O Lord, my prayer is your prayer
According to the plan of your salvation.
You save me,
You guard me by your mercy
Until the days of my sojourn end in peace.
You alone are my Savior now and forever.

O Lord,
I am for you,
So save me.

Psalm 7

Jesus – Our Song of Salvation

Lord Jesus Christ, save me from all the tribulation of life.
My tribulation is yours, because we are one.
You have been crucified and have risen
That we may have one life.
Therefore, I am not frightened if I face sadness and difficulties
Because you are victorious
And you want to be victorious by us
And in us.

Those who walk in the way of your love
May taste the tribulation of your cross,
But with it also is the glory and the majesty of your resurrection,
For you have not called us only to suffering and death
But also to life and salvation, in this place
Where there is suffering and death.

This is why my heart sings for you.
You, who became man for me,
That I may become a child for God.
I praise your name every day
Because your name is the song of my salvation.

Blessed are you, my Lord Jesus, because you hear my voice.
You even count the pulse of my heart,
That your heart and my heart may sing the same song of love.
Your love is freedom from every form of evil.
Blessed are you every day,
Your name is the song which cleanses my heart and my lips.
Hallelujah.

Psalm 8

Jesus, Your Name is the Glory of Humanity

Lord Jesus, your name is so precious to me,
More precious than my life.
It is my glory and my dignity to say, "Jesus is my Savior."
The glory of heaven was revealed at mount Tabor
When your beauty was revealed and inebriated the disciples,
Beauty that continues to overwhelm us at your holy table.

Lord Jesus, your glory is revealed in creation,
But also in the inner life of our humanity.
Your divine power created beauty and harmony for humanity.
When you planned to become incarnate
You lifted us higher than the angels,
Bestowing on us your beauty and holiness.
All that your divinity shared with your humanity,
For your love and goodness are infinite.

Lord Jesus, you gave us authority over all creation.
When it was lost by Adam,
You came to reveal that it is restored to us in you.
In your incarnation, you revealed your life and your authority
Over the water, the storms, the fish,
The unclean spirits and our diseases.
Truly, everything was submitted under your feet
Because you came to transfer us
From the slavery of the first Adam, to your freedom
And to the glory of your eternal kingdom,
For you are the second Adam.

O Son of God, glory be to you
With the Father and the Holy Spirit.

Psalm 9

Jesus Caught Me, to My Great Delight

Why have you have asked me to love you with an
Undivided heart,
And with an unwavering will,
And with a pure mind,
And that I seek you as the only pursuit of my life?
You asked this for my sake, so that I may find a joy
In your salvation that cannot be eclipsed.
That I may become more and more free from all
That distracts me and divides my heart,
From my past that lures me to return to my false life,
Seducing me away from true life.

But you are sitting on the throne of your divinity,
Bearing our humanity, at the right hand of the Father.
You have called me to sit next to you and share Your glory,
For you do not desire to keep anything for yourself.
You are good, you are perfect, and you are
Unenslaved to any needs, for you are the great Creator.
In your mercy, all of creation can find identity in you.

The Father looks at us, and sees us as members of your body.
The Holy Spirit looks at us with the same intimate love and
Compassion that he had when he anointed you at the river Jordan.
The Spirit has joy in you, and in you he has his joy in us.
He lives in us and knows our weakness,
Yet being one with you, he dwells in us as he dwells in you

You have liberated us from the tyranny of death
And brought us to the dwelling place of your holy church
That we may praise you with the heavenly powers
And glorify your holy name.

As for those who forget the beauty of your new covenant,

They will become subjected to the law
And never discover your love.
But you, Lord, can rescue them by your mercy
So that with them, we will all glorify you.
Most Holy Trinity,
Giver of salvation and grace to us all.

Psalm 10

Jesus' Bitter Labor Yields Glorious Fruit

I have walked with you to enter together
Into the garden of Gethsemane,
And with you I have lived the agony in the garden.
In my suffering, I have no one but you.
When you were in your agony in the garden,
Your best friends fell asleep
And you did not find comfort among your chosen.
Peter denied you;
Judas betrayed you.
These are two chapters written for all believers.

We have too many Peters and too many Judases in our churches.
But you, Lord Jesus, are not alone.
You were, and are, in the Father, anointed by the Holy Spirit.

We are besieged by our suffering under the siege of pain,
The betrayal of friends and
The blasphemies of our enemies.

And so the days of your life and death
Became like chapters in our life.
Even the death of those who believe in you
Became like your death.
But your resurrection and the glory of your ascension
Is the glorious end of those who are one with you.

Raise me, Lord, if I fall.
Because of the condemnation of those who hate me
And defame me,
You reject their condemnation.
It is the most loved song of Satan.
But you are the king of all the ages, and
I am with you until the end of time,

Crucified and risen in you
For your glory

Glory be to you,
Who made your cross an antidote for the fear of death,
For the healing of our souls from sin and the defilement of death,
Who made resurrection the fruit of the new life of humanity.

Psalm 11

Jesus – Lover of Mankind Calling Us to Our Senses

Only you have I trusted
Because you have been crucified for me.
I flee from the cunning designs of humans
To the shelter of your gospel,
Lest the wisdom of the world kill me
Or the craftiness and the treachery of humans poison my life.

You are alive in me
And you do not accept that I should turn my back on you.
Neither by my mind
Nor by my will
You look at me as you look at your humanity.
The same compassion and the same self-love you had for your life,
You also have for me.
You see my weakness as an opportunity
To work with me and in me
With the same pleasure you have for your own humanity.
Your eyes watch my wounds to give me medicine.

For you, darkness is like light
Because you are the Creator of night and day.
Your face will shine in the darkness of our time,
You will disperse all the wicked council of humans
Who walk according to the desires of their own hearts
And reject the wisdom of your cross.
Surely they will fall in the pit of their pride.

Those who reject your cross, reject your incarnation.
Those who reject your incarnation, will reject your resurrection.
And these will live like the deaf blind
Who have lost all sense of God's love for humanity.

But you, Lord, are the Lover of Mankind.

You wait for those who call upon you
To water the seed of love that you placed in them,
By the water of the Spirit.
So all may live by the water of the Spirit
And taste your infinite, unfathomable love.
Glory to you,
Our Good Savior.

Psalm 12

Jesus Put to Death the Condemnation of Death

Lord Jesus,
From the pulpit of our churches
We blaspheme you.
We make you a price being paid for our sins,
While you are our Co-Creator
With the Father and the Holy Spirit.

Give us wisdom and the tongue of love
That we may speak and live according to your love
And not fall into the love of the power of judgment.
The Evil will perish like all the ignorant
Who magnify their life and create their being by their own words.
But as we have received the gift of wisdom of the Spirit,
We shall re-create our being with you.

You Lord Jesus create us new every day,
For your love for our humanity is infinite
And we bind ourselves to this creative power
So that we may be saved.
May your name dwell in our hearts forever,
May your name become our song that leads us
To the communion of eternal life.

Your promises, Lord Jesus, are the manifestation of your person.
Our fathers accepted your promises, and put them into practice
And thus they lived by your life
And by your teaching in the church.

Your union with our humanity is my shelter.
It is not a word, or a page in a book,
But it is your incarnate divine life, defeating all obstacles.
Your life has established eternal union.
Glory be to you, Lord, because you govern all by love and truth.

Your truth is your love, your divine glory,
Your truth is sealed by your life-giving cross,
And by the light of your sacrificial love, which is your gift
For our eternal life.

When you gave life,
You slaughtered death and condemnation.

Psalm 13

Singing Jesus' Solidarity with Us

In my lonely nights, I remember your lonely nights,
And in my isolation where there is no friend
I remember you walking in hostile villages in Judea.

Being an alien, I have no company except you.
But you, Lord Jesus, are one with the Father,
And my union with you is the narrow road
That you have chosen for me.
The road that leads to salvation from all the
Temptations of the wide road.

Enlighten me by your divine presence
That I may see the beauty of eternal life
So that I may not be overcome by the mortality of my flesh
And the weakness of my perception.

I lean on your life-giving cross, for it is the shelter of my life.
My cry will always be that you will not leave me
Because you have pulled down all forms of separation
And obliterated isolation by your union with our humanity.

Therefore, I will praise your mercy,
Hymn your glorious love – love that lifted up
The downtrodden from the
Rubbish-heap of death, and from dust
Has lifted them to the glory of your divinity.

Psalm 14

Jesus – the Authentication of Our Humanity

I cannot leave you, Lord Jesus,
Because if I do, I have abandoned life.
If I forget you, I fall into the pit of the ignorance of my humanity
If I deny you, I deny eternal life.
But in my weakness, I cry out loud
With all the energy and the power I have,
"My Lord Jesus have mercy on me a sinner!"
Because my salvation is from you
And with you I have chosen my destiny.

The wisdom of human beings,
The councils of the wise of the earth who do not
Recognize your cross,
The ignorance of your cross,
Is a way of perdition

But the wisdom of your cross
And the power of your resurrection
Is life-giving to the poor,
Healing to the sick,
Resurrection for the broken.
For you do not snuff out a smoking wick
And you do not break a bruised reed.

In your death and resurrection, you had a taste of our weakness.
You drank the cup of our life to liberate us from mortality
And to transform us to your life by the power of the Holy Spirit.
Glory be to you, giver of wisdom,
Revealing the Father to us by the life-giving Spirit.

Psalm 15

Jesus' Glory of Self-Giving

Lord Jesus,
I love the beauty of your church,
The sanctuary where you dwell,
The altar where you reveal your sacrificial love for us
In the divine service.

You call us, we who are impure,
To purify our being
So as to praise you not by our tongues alone,
But also by the whole of our being.
The love that you have granted us is the true spring of our praise.

Our lips have touched your holy blood
In the chalice of your covenant
And our mouths have consumed the bread of life,
Which is glowing with the fiery love of your self-giving,
Which shines, seeking sinners.

Lord Jesus, your eternal covenant is joy and pleasure to our hearts.
Therefore, we praise you
With the Father who gave you to us,
And with the Holy Spirit,
Who revealed your union with us.

Psalm 16

Jesus – Our Eternal and Everlasting Inheritance

Protect me, Lord Jesus,
For I am your inheritance and your body.
You are my brother, my Savior and my Lord.
You have united me to the communion of your saints
Because it is your pleasure and comes out of your goodness.
You have brought me to your communion with the Father
And the Holy Spirit.
I will not abandon you,
Lest death should creep on me.
For you do not abandon anyone
Who cries out to your name,
Who beseeches your goodness and mercy.

My Lord Jesus,
You are my fortress and my life,
The shelter of my soul and my body,
My eternal inheritance.
You have chosen me before the creation of the world
And by your pleasure.
I come to you
To abide in you,
And you in me,
Forever

Our eternal union has no separation,
Its foundation is in your incarnation.
This is where you have united your divinity and your humanity,
Forever.

Glory be to you.
Glory for your love for humanity,
Love that does not reject anyone.

Glory be to you good Father, who gave your
Lord Christ Jesus to us.

Glory be to your Holy Spirit
Who dwells in us to unite us with you,
And with the Father,
Forever.

Psalm 17

Jesus – Our Glimpse of Fiery Love

My heart and my tongue ponder your promises.

I praise you for your indwelling in us.
From that indwelling in our hearts,
We taste the sweetness of your love.
Our hearts begin to sing praise.

You long to hear our prayer.
It comes from members of your body –
The beat of hearts, which you watch.
You hear us, rejoicing in our presence.
Your infinite love meets our little love
Like the waves of the sea that embrace a drop of water
Or a song of one bird.
In the midst of thousands of singing birds,
It is you, Lord Jesus, who move
So rapidly
So fiercely
Toward us.
Because of infinite love,
Because we are your body,
Which you long to unite with yourself.
Because we are
Your eternal inheritance.

Psalm 18

Jesus – the Pleasure of Serving

Lord Jesus Christ, you are my strength, my unshaken rock.
Your name is my fort.
It is not a name in my mind that my tongue utters,
But your name is the covenant of love and is your person.
I utter your name to become aware of your person.

Your love and your mercy protect me
Because you are my salvation,
The head of the church.

You are the mediator who rescued us from the pit of death,
Who saved us from damnation for the sake of your name's glory,
Who poured out fountains of your love because of your goodness.

You have seen the suffering of our humanity,
Our pain, our temptation, and our hard life.
You came to us and walked in the valley of death,
Enlightened us by your resurrection,
Rescued us from the claws of death.

You saved us because your pleasure is in humanity,
Which you created with the Father and the Spirit.
You freely give, to all, the eternal inheritance of your kingdom.

You are the giver of mercy.
You sealed your mercy by the blood of your cross,
A seal that cannot be erased
Because forever you are the Lover of Humanity.

My Lord Jesus Christ, glory be to you.

Psalm 19

Jesus – Giver of Life in Spite of Illness and Death

Although the sky is so infinite,
It cannot be compared to the magnitude of your love.
The glory of the cosmos is merely one beam of your glory.
All that you have created witnesses to your goodness,
All living visible things swim in the sea of your goodness.

Your incarnation testifies to your love for humanity.
Your cross is the crown of your love.

By your death you have abolished death,
And by your resurrection, the beauty of your love of
Humanity is shining forever.

Keep me, Lord, in your way, because it is the only way to life.
You have founded it by the humility of your love
And by your coming down from heaven to us
And by giving us a communion
In the eternal covenant of your love.

Not with words have you established this covenant,
But by water, Spirit, and blood –
The three witnesses of your commitment.
To wash us from the defilement of sin and death,
To liberate us from our slavery to our former nature,
To prepare us to become the free children
Of your heavenly kingdom.

Lord Jesus,
You are the purpose of my life
And the destiny of my being.

Psalm 20

Jesus – Our Sweet Communion

My soul suffers from being away from your presence.
Send your Spirit to help me quickly and bring me back
To our communion with you.

I am yours, Christ,
Whom you anointed by the Holy Spirit.
Your inheritance,
Whom you have chosen forever.

Remember Lord, our meetings at your altars.
How we receive you into our being, Lord and Savior,
When you offer yourself to us as the bread of life
And the cup of your love.

When I remember the service in which you offer yourself to us,
My tears come like a flood.
For every moment I am away from you
Causes tremendous sadness to me.
Lord, I am yours.
Save me from all that distracts my love.

Hear my cry when I call on you, my King,
For I have no other Savior but you.

Psalm 21

Jesus' Overwhelming Gift of Love

Lord Jesus, you made me a king in your eternal kingdom –
How can I not rejoice in remembering your mercy
That is so high above my perception and my understanding?
Who can unfold your hidden and mysterious plan
Or investigate your call?
For you have called us to share the glory of your divine life.

You called me, and then you washed me from my defilement,
Anointed me with the oil of Chrism,
Prepared a banquet for the Bread of Life
And the cup full of salvation and grace by which
You revive my mortal life,
Converting me from the slavery of nature
To the freedom of a person.

Who can explain your eternal love?
My heart is flooded with thanksgiving
Because your mercy is above what a tongue can express.
My life is established by the Holy Spirit,
Who does not fluctuate, but is always good,
And who does not hesitate to offer help for those who call for it.

By your cross I ascend to the vision of your love
In order to live it by your resurrection,
And remain in that vision by the power of your Holy Spirit.
My Lord Jesus Christ, glory be to you.

Psalm 22

Jesus Judges Death to Give Us Life

My God, my Lord, my Jesus, who tasted the
Darkness of death on the cross.
The judgment of death passed through your being
And as it met your life, it was abolished.

I have united myself with your cross day and night,
Lest the power of the world should overcome me.
I am crucified to the world,
I count myself as dead to it.

I shall seek nothing but your love
Because I have left everything to seek the eternal treasure
Buried in the field of your goodness.
Therefore, I will not be shaken when I seek you

My God, my God, you are my salvation!
My delight is to call you my God.
For my sake you have drunk the cup of death
That I may drink the cup of life.
The whole of my being calls upon you.
My soul and my body confess your divinity
Because you have touched both of them
And have given life to both.

You are my shelter, the fortification of my being.
You have been crucified for my sake.
Glory be to you, who are of the Father,
You who invest us with the power of the Holy Spirit,
My Jesus.

Psalm 23

Jesus – the Good Shepherd

Lord Jesus, the Good Shepherd,
You gave your life for the sheep.
You died for us sinners to give life by your resurrection.
You are my king who gave me a share in your Kingdom
And made all of us kings, to rule with you forever.

You lead us to your divine communion with your Father.
You comfort us with the indwelling of the Comforter.
The Spirit of the Father who anointed you in Jordan,
Anoints us eternally

Because of your great unspeakable love,
You have prepared the Table of Manna and the Cup of your Love
For us to eat the Bread of Life and drink your blood
And live forever with you and with the Father by your Spirit.

Great Shepherd, who loves us and gives us life,
Your Life,
We will not fear the darkness of the grave.
You will give us rest from this earthly life,
You will renew us for the heavenly one.

Thus we will walk in this life with you, our Shepherd,
And sing praises to your holy name
And bless your Father and the Holy Spirit.

We will dwell with you in the Godhead,
Waiting for the perfection of our dwelling.
We see it now in your coming to serve us in the Divine Liturgy.
Halleluiah.

Psalm 24

Jesus – the Creator Who Became Human

My Lord Jesus, you are the creator of heaven and earth.
You have created all that exists
And without you nothing can exist,
For all creation receives existence from you.

You founded everything by your goodness
And by your compassion,
You have cared for creation as a shepherd.
All living creatures receive a spark of your mercy.

By your incomprehensible incarnation,
We human beings exist in your divine, incarnate life.
We are in you
And you are in us,
Leading us from glory to glory
That at the end we will sit with you
On your divine throne in heaven.

Merciful Almighty, the wounds in my soul are mortal,
But you have my medicine, and you alone can administer it
Because you are life and you are the resurrection.
King of Glory,
Crowned on my heart as the king of the whole universe,
Glory be to you.

Psalm 25

Jesus – Our Shared Immortality

Lord Jesus Christ,
Crucified for my sake,
You drank the cup of death
That I may drink the cup of life.
How can I put my trust in someone else?
While no one else, except you, is life.

Your way is the way of the incarnation and the cross.
Incarnate to share
And crucified to remove death that hinders us from sharing.
Your way is your unique love that keeps nothing but gives all.
Sustain me by this power of sacrificial love
Which has crushed our death
And has nailed life, with the nails of love, into our mortal life
To unify us with your immortal life.

Have mercy on me
Because I am your flesh and I am your brother.
My tribulations are your tribulation.
This is why I wait for you.

The darkness of Calvary did not stay for long.
The silence of the grave could not keep your life.
The dawn of the resurrection sprang like light,
Taking away the gloom of pain and death.

My Lord, you are the Savior.
In you alone do I put my trust.

Psalm 26

Jesus – the Divine Plan of Our Perfection

Lord Jesus, you are my perfection, for you give me eternal life.
You complete my creation,
You love me and prepare me to be your inheritance.

You completed the plan of our salvation
By being first born of the virgin.
You have perfected our salvation
By uniting our body to your divinity,
And when you united us in your death
You abolished our death
And granted us immortality by your resurrection
To keep us forever in communion with you
And the Father and the Holy Spirit.
So you became the plan of my life.
You are the only way to true life.
Therefore, I praise you with all of your saints.

I have seen what you have done
With Moses the Black
And with Mary of Egypt.
The glory of these, the martyrs of your love,
Brings strength to my will.
In the midst of all of the saints
I praise you.

Psalm 27

Jesus – Gift of New Eternal Delight

Lord Jesus, your life is the light of my life.
You are the cause of my existence.
You have illuminated me by the light of your teaching
And by your death and your resurrection.
You are my salvation, because you are the covenant
Of the eternal love.
You abolished the condemnation of death,
Therefore, I do not fear the hatred of people
Or those who revile me,
For you are my hope, the Lord Almighty.

Your peace has given me life,
O King of Peace.
You are my eternal dwelling,
You are my eternal pleasure.
The joy of my life that will not diminish
For my new being is from you
And by you.

I have been born a new birth in holy baptism.
Bless O Lord, my father and my mother,
Who gave me my biological birth,
And reward them by eternal goodness.
But keep us together in your eternal love
That we may have communion with you
And have our share in your heavenly inheritance.
Your kingdom of the Father and the Spirit,
Glory be to you, Holy Trinity, our true God.

Psalm 28

Jesus is the Covenant of Eternal Inheritance

All of my being calls upon you
Because I am your inheritance,
And you cannot forget your body.

For you have counted the hair of my head
And told their number to your Holy Father,
And you have fixed the days of my life
Because you are my Creator.

You are my majesty,
The rock of my being.

Save your church from its affliction
Because it is your dwelling on earth.

Blessed are you Lord
Who have chosen us before the foundation of the world
To become your eternal inheritance.

Psalm 29

Song of the Transformation of our Humanity

The heavenly powers see me in your presence
And they glorify you for your mercy and your grace.
Your love of an earthly creature is so amazing,
No tongue can explain.

You hear my voice, O Lord.
The words I use to call out to you,
You have given them to me.
I cry out to you in my longing
That you may quench my thirst
By the water of your mercy.
You pour out your pleasure on me
Because I carry your image.

All heavenly invisible powers glorify you
Because of the greatness of your humility.
That which moved you to take our earthly being
And transform it to the heavenly and the divine.

Psalm 30

Jesus – Lover of Man

Glory be to you,
Lover of Man.
You who give up your divine glory,
Becoming human like us, apart from sin.

Glory be to you
In your holy sanctuary,
At your altars where your Holy Spirit
Descends to give us the bread of life;
And you, Lord of Glory, come to us
Distributing your most holy body and blood,
Calling us by your voice to eat and to drink;
And by your hands, distributing your life to us,
You are life and no one can give your life to us, except you.

By your love you unify us with you
And make us a living sacrifice to witness to your love.
When your life penetrates our being
And your peace dwells in our heart,
All the difficulties of our life become like a dream.

O King of Peace,
Enthroned and carried by the cherubim,
You declare your great love to us humans.
You sanctify us.
We call upon your name
As you call us by our names
To participate in your grace.

Glory be to you,
Lover of Man.

Psalm 31

Jesus – Our Eternal Anointing and Eternal Dwelling

I glorify your name, O Lord,
Because you have glorified me
With the glory of the grace of adoption.

You have liberated me, O Lord,
From the slavery of death and sin.
Destroyed the power of hell.
Released the captives there.
Shattered the power of death.
Abolished the curse of the law.

And made me one with you.

You have changed my life from the darkness of slavery
To the glory of your freedom.
You anointed me with your Holy Spirit,
An eternal unction for eternal dwelling,
That I may become a holy sanctuary in which you dwell forever.

I glorify you, my Lord Jesus Christ.
Forever and forever I will confess your name,
For I have no other Savior but you.

Psalm 32

Jesus, Unhindered in His Love

Your incarnation made you like me.
I trust in you,
And on your cross
I lean.
And by the power of your resurrection,
I shall live.

You Lord Jesus are the rock of my life.
In the affliction of this life,
You are with me.
You do not permit the waves of afflictions to drown me.
Neither does my disgrace please you.

In your hands are all the days of my life,
For you even count them.
The light of your divinity goes ahead of me every day of my life.
Your light surrounds me to keep me in communion with you.
It shines inside me to give me understanding.

You enlighten the darkness of my life as you reveal to me
My deepest intentions that are hidden from my eyes
So that I will not be lost.
You hold my hand
So I cannot turn my back to you.
If I fall, you raise your servant
And renew my hope in your mercy
And in owning your inheritance.

You shared my humanity because of your great goodness
And fortified my being through the eternal origin of my new life.
You put on me the garment of your righteousness –
Not to cover up my mortality, but to mingle your life with my life,
That I may become like you.

You gave me a place to sit, with you, on your divine throne
Forever.

My heart rejoices in you
And praises your name always.
For truly, you have become the song of my life.

Psalm 33

Jesus – the Freedom of Slaves

I glorify you O Lord
Because you became human for our sake.

O my God, we did not ask you to become human
But you freely chose to become human to save us,
To lift us from the pit of slavery, to the glory of your freedom.
You made us one with you,
Free children of your Father.

You have lifted up the tyranny of death,
Crashing judgment under your feet,
Raising us from the death of sin to new life,
Transforming us from slaves to free children,
From death to eternal life.

Therefore, my heart will never cease
Nor will my tongue ever be silent,
But I shall glorify you and confess your great salvation –
The gift, which you give
To all those who believe and call upon you.

Psalm 34

Jesus is Our Assurance

Blessed are you Lord,
For you have forgiven all my trespasses
And have not counted even one single sin.
Thus, I will not hide anything from you,
Lest I return to my old life and forsake you.
I confess to you all my thoughts
So that you may liberate me from them.
Not one single idea can dominate my being,
Not one single desire can overpower me.
You are my life that cannot be separated from me.
You come to my help.
Because your compassion is not held back by my trespasses,
Neither do you treat me according to my thoughts,
Nor protect me according to my readiness to follow you,
But only according to your mercy.

By your love and your goodness,
You protect me.
My weakness will not take control of me.
You are the way that I must take,
Carrying my cross to follow you
So that all your saints may rejoice in me,
And with them, all of heaven.
I remain in communion with you.

My Lord Jesus Christ,
You are my forgiveness
And my life.

Psalm 35

Jesus – Revealer and Giver of the Father's Mercy

All of your holy and saintly angels
Rejoice because I became a member of your body,
Walking in the way of your life,
Carrying my cross,
Singing the song of victory.
The new life has dawned on us.

You have filled the whole universe with your mercy
And the light of your resurrection has shined on us.
You have created everything.
You did not abandon anything to decay.
No, instead you came and saved all from death,
Restored all to the divine image

By your word,
Heaven and earth were created.
Still, your love was not revealed by word,
But by flesh and blood.
By this love we shall live,
Feeding on your word.
Everything you see will exist
And what we choose to give from your holiness
Will become our inheritance.
Therefore, our hearts rejoice in you
And the song of our life is your sweet name

My Lord Jesus,
The revealer and the giver of the mercy of God the Father,
In you alone we trust.

Psalm 36

Jesus' Name Is the Divine Plan

I find your name sweeter than honey,
More precious than my life.
I fortify myself with your name in order to live.
I boast in your name
That your mercy may dwell in my heart.
I call upon your name, which you love, for your name is your joy
Which makes known your love for humanity.
When I utter your name,
My tongue and my heart are at the peace you have bestowed.

You are our peace and our salvation and the joy of our souls.
By your name, we participate in the praise of your love
And join your heavenly beings
And glorify you with your saints.
You spread the light of your mercy
And the whole creation lives by your grace.
You hear those who call upon you
Because you cannot forget your body.
Your heavenly angels will come and set their camp around us.
Thus, we will lack nothing.

Goodness is in the communion of your love.
If we forsake your love, we shall truly perish.
When you see a small spark of love in us,
You hasten to make it perfect
So that it may reach its goal – which is eternal communion.

My Lord Jesus,
You are my Creator and my Savior.
All those who trust in you will grow up
In the communion of your Holy Spirit.

Psalm 37

Jesus is the Revelation of Triune Love

Lord, hasten to my help.
Keep pouring your love into my being.
For I am thirsty for you.
I was distracted away from you, and nearly abandoned you.
I found myself empty, being created out of nothing.
Death was creeping upon me
But when I remembered your name,
The name of my salvation and of my life,
I called upon you
So that I would not fall into the pit of sadness.

I remembered how you united yourself to my humanity.
My soul was comforted
Because your divinity never was separated
From my humanity in you.
But my sadness was too much.
The burdens of my heart
Nearly made me forget you.
Drowned in the waves of my thoughts,
I became alone and poor.

But your Spirit moved in my heart
With the meekness of the Comforter.
He spoke to me
Stirred up my hope
And ignited the fire of my longing.
I became thirsty for you.
This is the hidden, deep pain in my heart that will never go away:
I feel, I perceive, your love, but I miss its fullness.
When I cry that you pour the fullness of your love in me,
I know that my fragile being could not take it.
I can bear only a little of your love.

You have judged us.
The verdict was eternal righteousness
Declared by your divine incarnation.
The verdict was sealed by your life-giving blood.
The verdict was made eternal by your resurrection.
Therefore, I shall dwell in that triune hope,
Praising you, Lord Jesus,
As my life and my eternity
Until the day of my full unity with you.

Psalm 38

Jesus' Love Redefines Judgment

My Lord Jesus,
You have only one way:
It is the way of love and goodness
Where God and humanity are united.
Evil is the shame that you do not accept.
That is why you wash our souls
Until all are clean and pure
In the day of your majesty.

On the day of your great judgment,
The day in which you come with your glory
To reveal your power,
To separate the goats from the sheep,
You judge by love –
Which you have revealed in yourself
In healing and in forgiveness.

Your justice brought me back to your way
Because the way of evil is darkness –
Bitterness to anyone who has tasted the sweetness of your gospel.
The river of your grace overflows in our churches.
From the founts of baptism, we are born and sanctified
And at the table we meet you as king, distributing your life to us.
We receive you and you receive us,
For you are the resurrection and the life eternal.
By your light we shall see the light,
Revealing to us the meaning of the Scriptures.
The Father, who gave you as a gift to us,
Plants in us the great gift of adoption.

Your mercy is forever
Because you do not forsake those
Whom you have made your body,

Those who are one with you.

Glory be to you, my Lord Jesus.

Psalm 39

Jesus Became Mortal for Our Sake

You did not unite yourself to our humanity for your own sake,
But for our sake.
You defined the way of our union by your union
With our humanity.
This is the way of life.
When you died freely,
You united your will to the will of the Father
And by accepting death in your flesh, you abolished separation.
For sacrificing our will in communion with you
Will preserve our life.
Whoever finds his life
Will close the door of life on his heart.
But whoever gives his life in love for you
Will find the fruit of your love in him
And in the other members of your body.
For your sake, and only by you, we become spiritual sacrifices.
Sacrificed in order to live with you
And die with you
In order that we may rise with you.
If we die without you, our death will be the death of sin
And the victory of our nature over your love and mercy.
If we live without you, our life will be only
A biological life that will rot.

Purify my heart from all hidden desires
In order that I may be free from them
And be totally for you.
You are my eternal inheritance,
My Lord Jesus.
Therefore, confirm my steps when I walk in your way
That I may not abandon the way of love.
For you have planned this way as the only way to life.
If I turn from it, I will fall into the pit of evil.

You alone are the Savior.
The wisdom of humanity is all vanity
Because only your wisdom is declared in your humility.
In self-emptying, you revealed true power
And true love for sinners.
And when you renew all sinners,
Your love will have truly triumphed.

My heart has clung to your words
That I may live according to your image.
My soul has received your peace.
It was seeking your image.
When your image was discovered,
I unified myself with your image.

O Lord, all my yearning for you will not be forgotten.
It is a thirst for a perfect love.
Your grace sustains me,
Qualifies me for your glorious resurrection,
That I may participate in your glory.
O Lord, glory be to you.

Psalm 40

Jesus is Our Savior, Divine and Human

My sins appear to me
Like a nightmare that has gone by
Because the light of your love for sinners
Has shunned and dispersed all the nightmares of my life.
You love me in spite of all of my failings
And in spite of all of my deviation from your way,
Your love always brings me back to you.

Your love is my eternal hope that will not be shaken.
You stretch out your hand with help, invisibly,
To those who are in despair.
But those who have just a spark of hope
Can see it.
You strengthen those who are weak
By participating in carrying our burden,
And by your participation
You plant the cross of your love in our hearts.
When it is planted,
It becomes a cross for each one of us according to our growth.

Humans make themselves my enemy
And mock your love,
Saying that you are only human and deny your divinity.
Truly, by denying your divinity, they deny also your humanity.
Because without your divinity,
We cannot understand your humanity.
And without your humanity,
We cannot understand your divinity
For you are the one divine incarnate Savior.
The human who has taken all that belongs to us, except our sins.
Only God can do this.
You came like a physician to heal us.
Your holiness comforts my soul.

Your holiness does not separate you from me
Or me from you.
You are the holy one of the Father
Who became man in order to dwell among us,
To sanctify us.
You did not keep your holiness to yourself, but kept it for us
So that we may participate in your holiness.

Your love and your tenderness have defeated our bitterness.
So much so that you take no account of our thoughts
Because you do not judge us by our thoughts,
You do not judge us at all,
Because you came as a Savior –
Not as a judge.

Glory be to you in all your doings.

Psalm 41

Jesus – Our Hymn of New Life

If only my tongue could speak your words –
And only your words –
And be silent,
Not uttering any other word
So that I may keep the fire of your love in my heart
And not scatter my love by a discourse about anything else.

Without you I am only a shadow without life.
My days are counted as a limited time that will pass away.
But in you I am alive forever.
There is no end for my life
Because you are my life.
Therefore, you have become the hope that can defeat
All the difficulties of my life.

True shame is to abandon you.
What is regarded as lofty and great
Is abomination compared with your love.
You guide me with your mercy in order that I may not lose you

Come to me to heal me
Because I am your body.
You have carried the burden of humanity
Healed our nature from the wound of pride.
Pride is the true enemy of all that is good.
It is the false judge that you have judged.
When we judge others, we create trials for them
And we pass verdicts of death.
You judge our life in that we have not loved you
Or understood your mercy or love for sinners.

My Lord Jesus,
May your cross be my tongue, my lips, and my silence also,

For your cross is life and medicine,
Way and light.
Your cross has gathered together your incarnation
And your resurrection
Because your death became life
And your incarnation became union with us
And your resurrection became eternal life.
All these have gathered in you,
In the sign of salvation, the cross.
O I wish that my tongue and my heart
Will be crucified with you
So that I will not utter anything but your name,
And that I may live in the light of your love.

Psalm 42

Jesus – Song of Shared Love

Jesus, you long for me,
Because in your incarnate being is my humanity.

My longing meets yours
And my thirst for you meets your thirst for me.

You did not will to be the Only-Begotten,
But designed with the Father to be the first-born
Among many brothers.
O giver of the grace of adoption,
It is this grace that made you and us one sanctuary.

In the midnight prayer,
I pass over, through your promises,
Not to a land,
But to the plan of your salvation.
For I have no promised land
But I have the promise of the Father
Who has been poured out on Pentecost.
I alienate myself from you by my mind,
But my heart is in pain
Because in your presence
I stand in the gathering of the saints who renounced the world
In order to sing with them
And glorify your abundant grace.
I meet you at your holy altar
Where is the memory of your self-giving,
Your first love, which you planted in the ocean of my heart,
And the icons of the saints tell me
That one day I will be glorified like them.
I see the great Anthony
And those who have mastered wisdom and love
And courage and discernment.

And though I have no place among them
I find, in infinite love and mercy,
That my true place is your Divine Person,
Where my humanity is united to your divinity.

Jesus,
You are my salvation and the rock
On which you have established my new being.
You are my God
Because you still give your life in every liturgy.
Early in the morning, I join the heavenly choir
Of the cherubim and seraphim
In order that I may receive a living call of your fiery love,
That my being may become inflamed with your love,
Which you give to those who do not deserve.

Thank you, Lord, the God of my salvation.
Because of what you have revealed
In the life of your saints,
Making each one of them a chapter
In the book of your infinite love.

Psalm 43

Jesus – the Judge of Death

Lord Jesus, you have judged death as useless and aimless
So you annihilated our death by your life-giving death.
What a paradox to put death to death, by accepting death
To end its tyranny over us.

Your resurrection is the verdict of eternal life,
And so you became my fortress that shelters humanity from death.
You also became the spring of eternal life.
The light of your incarnation guides me
To your union with our humanity.

Therefore, whenever I am troubled
I remember that you became human for our sake
In order to reveal your union with us.
Your cross judged sin and death.
This comforts my life when the fear of death troubles me.
O my Lord, you are a river of life and forgiveness.

I come to you while yet you are everywhere,
Even resting in the hearts of those who seek you.

I contemplated your dwelling place in our sanctuaries.
There, in the baptistery and at your table
Where we are born and nourished by the food of immortality,
A breath of your Spirit penetrated my being,
United me to your love, even a sinner like me.

How great is your goodness and your generosity,
Lord Jesus, my God and my Savior.
Praise and thanksgiving be to you
With the Father and the Holy Spirit.

Psalm 44

Jesus Shares Our Human Body

Lord Jesus Christ,
I have heard and seen your work in the saints of the church,
In Antony, Macarius, and Pachomius,
And I have contemplated the witness of Athanasius
And the blood of our martyrs
Who loved you to death, refusing to deny your name
Because of their great love for you.
Because of them, I throw myself at your feet
Begging that I may have participation in the life of your saints,
That I may have the honesty of Anthony,
The integrity of Macarius,
The wisdom of Pachamious,
And the witness of Athanasius.
That I may stand with them in your presence in your eternal glory.

Lord Jesus, look at me!
Without you I am poor and I will end in nothingness.
But you have rescued me from the pit of ignorance
And from the darkness of hatred, you have liberated me.
The light of the life of your saints is shining in my heart.
This light has your light
And you have given me a share in it.
I have learned from them how to follow your steps,
But without you I cannot complete my journey with you.

For the sake of the glory of your name,
Shine upon us by the light of your face
And renew the face of our community
That we may become, truly, your living body
And the true witness of redemption and salvation of humanity.
O Lord Jesus, you are my hope and my strength.

Psalm 45

The Taste of Your Love, Jesus, is Like Fire in my Heart

O my Lord, you have filled my heart with thanks
For your grace has overflowed.
It has succeeded to purify my filth.
The whole cosmos became so small compared to your love
Which draws me to you.
Who can compare the rays of your mercy
With anything that we can see?
For you are the Creator of all beauty and the giver of wisdom,
But you are greater than all the beauty you have ever created.
You are the eternal wisdom that shines with love.

My tongue speaks, but my words are constrained
By what I perceive
For I am limited by my vocabulary.
But when I am quiet and stop talking,
My heart burns inside me with your love
And incites me to praise you.
But praising you also calls me to silence.

By your great glory, which you poured over humanity
As you made us co-heirs with you,
You lead us to the heavenly, eternal throne.
How marvelous is the destiny of our life,
For we are born of the wombs of our mothers
In order to inherit your eternal kingdom.
From the mud of the earth, you bring forth the bread of eternal life
And from the graves, you lift us up to the glory of the heavens.
For all of this we glorify you,
The one with the Father and the Spirit.

You have sealed humanity with your Spirit,
All glory and praise to the Holy Trinity, hallelujah.
The Lord is my Savior and my strength.

Psalm 46

Jesus – Song of Hope and Firm Assurance

O Jesus, you are my strong fortress,
The only help,
The only one who was crucified for humanity.
By your cross, you have revealed the end of every power.
Even if the earth is shaken or the mountains are upturned,
You remain enthroned in your humility and in our humanity.
Thus, our humanity remains enthroned in you.
All that is around us is changing, lacking stability,
For every creature without you cannot sustain itself.
But you, Lord, have every power in your right hand!
The same right hand that you stretched out for the nails
On the cross
To abolish death;
The same hand that destroyed the grave and captured hell
And shone out with immortality.
O Lord Jesus, your strength is my love
And your love is my strength.
You are the hope
Because you are the head of the church which cannot be severed,
For truly the church is your body.
Hallelujah.

Psalm 47

Jesus is Our Root of Eternal Life

All of our saints rejoice in you
Because, though mortal, they have received your grace,
And those who were born of the womb are now born of the Father.
You became human that we may become your brothers and sisters.

Everything is under your feet,
Even death and judgment,
For you abolished the power of sin,
Made the sting of the Law blunt.
You sit as incarnate on the throne of divinity
So all humanity is seated with you
In order that you may gather together all humans
Into your eternal kingdom.

We praise you for your grace that shines forth
In the dark night of our death.
It is the light of your resurrection
Which leads us to know the Father through you.

We praise you for the beauty of your cross,
The creative power of redemption that has liberated us.
It has taken my spirit captive
And you have captivated even your Spirit to dwell in our souls,
Comforting us,
Lifting us to the glory of your son-ship.

Lord Jesus Christ, glory be to you.

Psalm 48

Jesus – Our Sanctuary

Great are you, Lord Jesus, because of your incarnation.
Praised because of your glorious redemption,
Glorified by your resurrection and by forming your church
From your holy body, by the Holy Spirit.

From your bones and your flesh, you made us a new creation,
And because of your great love, you made us your body.
By the power of salvation, you keep us united with you
As you have united your divinity to our humanity.
Your holy church is the city of the holy Trinity
Where your Father and the Holy Spirit are enthroned
To grant your body, the church, your eternal beauty.

In your holy sanctuary, you offer us your life
The holy offering of your body and your blood.
You truly love your body,
But your self-love is a sacrificial love
Uniting you and us in the one body, your church
To become one with you and in you forever.

Blessed are you Lord Jesus Christ, from now to eternity.

Psalm 49

Jesus without Our Definitions

O Jesus,
What humans can say about your love will never frighten me.
The discourse of the learned seems so convincing
But does not explain the mystical power of your love –
That power which penetrates the hearts quietly and even silently
With the silence of your humility
Until you capture our hearts.

You took me captive without chains.
True freedom is that which is not subjected to the laws of nature,
And that is you –
You who have no nature that could subject you to its laws,
For subjection to nature is the very character of all that is created.
But your created-ness is glorified in your divinity.

You are free in your love,
Generous to the extent that you even gave up your being
To give us life, the opposite of death,
Which we brought upon ourselves.
Death, you have trampled under your feet on the cross.
The grave could not contain you, O Free One,
Nor could the underworld take you captive.
For you enlightened the whole creation by the light of your life
In order to establish a new creation out of the old one.

Your plan of salvation is above everything
That a tongue can express.
When we defined you by our definitions, we lost you.
When we besieged you by our intellectual theories,
Which are the chains of our mortal nature,
We were not able to see you.
Your freedom, we could not understand
Due to our long enslavement.

We think that freedom is a choice between two things,
But the free choice of love is not restricted to two or three.

The freedom of your love has no boundaries.
It does not take what is agreeable and reject what is disagreeable;
It puts under foot all the acceptable, and even all the possible,
And does the impossible,
Because the choice of self-giving is to give to the unworthy.
What is more, it is to give what does not belong
To the entire universe
But only to your being,
To give your body and blood.

You passed over to us in flesh and blood
In order that the richness of your divinity
May pass over to us who are poor and deprived even of life.
Truly you have taken what belongs to us
And have given to us what belongs to you.
By taking what belongs to us, you became one with us,
And by giving what belongs to you, you made us one with you.

I love you, my Lord Jesus,
My strength and my life,
The song of my present and my next life.

Psalm 50

Jesus – Song of Mercy and Forgiveness

Have mercy on me, my Lord Jesus,
According to the great mercy that you revealed
To the prostitute who was caught in her sins
And to the thief who was crucified with you.

Have mercy on me according to your immense compassion
Which wiped out the sin of Peter
And even warned Judas.

Wash me thoroughly, just as you washed the feet of your disciples.
Wash my heart that I may be transfigured
By the grace of your Holy Spirit.

Count me as the sheep on your right hand.
Because you have sealed me with the royal seal of your Holy Spirit.

Give me the joy and the strength of your resurrection,
That my soul may rejoice in the gift of eternal life.
I magnify your mercy and your love for sinners,
O Lover of Man.

Psalm 51

Jesus, Your Name is the Song of Love

I sleep and your name is on my lips
So that when I wake up, I find your name is in my heart.
Your name is the first thing I utter, to begin the day as our day.
Your name is the only good that I know.
It has reconciled me with my life, and with my enemies also,
For you are the Savior who established peace within humanity.

Your name is the divine truth incarnate,
Revealed in our time, and every language became like light –
Light that shines in the darkness of our life.

Your name is sealed with your blood.
It is the only name that has been washed by the blood of its owner;
It is the only name that has shined with the light of immortality
By your resurrection;
It is the only immortal name that we know
Coined from our human letters.
All of our names will perish, except your name,
While we are waiting to receive the new name.
All new names will carry the seal of your love.

Your name is the song of my love,
It is my patience and my endurance.
Your name is my discipline,
So when I utter it, I am united with you.
Every drop of my blood cries out.
O Jesus, you are my life.

Psalm 52

Jesus is the Flood of the Father's Love

O Jesus,
You are the offering of eternal love
Offered to us by the Father.
You are also the bread of the Father that came down from heaven
To give life to our humanity.

O flood of love that has no boundaries,
You became human.
You united yourself to our humanity,
Each part of our body became a member of your body.
You raised our humanity to your immortal life
Because you truly love humanity.

At the altar of your offering, we meet
Every day and every hour of our time.
But the true altar of your offering is your good will,
The will that accepted to die for the sinful and the immoral.
Eternal, and manifested in time,
Your will became a river full of your life.

You are the altar, and the offering,
And the church in its eternal beauty,
For the fullness of divinity dwells in you.
To gather around you the poor, who do not know the true divinity,
Your body is the place of your divinity
And your divinity is the place of our humanity.

And whoever separates your divinity from your humanity
Will have neither.
And by such separation
The gift of adoption and the kingdom are lost.

But you, my Lord, are the incarnate God

Who came to destroy separation,
To defeat all powers of separation in all of its forms.
For you came to unite us with you and the Father by the Spirit.

O Jesus, the offering of my life,
The bread of my life,
The cup of my existence.
My words have dried up, and my speech has stumbled
Because the flood of your grace is too much to be expressed.
Glory be to you in everything.

Psalm 53

Jesus, Your Cross Is a Sign of Life

I signed my chest with the sign of your cross.
My chest became your church.
I signed my heart with the sign of your cross.
My heart became your altar.
I sign my lips with the sign of your cross
That my speech may become a witness to you.
The sign of your cross is you.
Where you sign us with your life,
You open to us the doors of the freedom of choice.
But your sign does not shackle us.
You give us the freedom of love.

Psalm 54

Jesus – Our Cup of Love

Your blood calls my blood in order to be one blood.
A blood of one witness
That Jesus is Lord
To the glory of God the Father.
I do not redeem myself with my blood
Because you alone are the redeemer and the redemption.
Your blood calls my blood
Because our love is one love, one blood, one life.

Your cross is not only a word on the tongue of a preacher
Or drops in a cup of the supper.
Rather, it is the offering of life.
Take and drink, this is my blood
Which we shed when we bend down to serve others,
When a mother is giving her breast to her newly born baby.
It fills your cup with blood.
And when a farmer goes out to plow his field,
Your cup is full of grace
For those who will eat the produce of the field.
When two meet in the bond of marriage to become one body
Your blood has reached its goal.
That is the unification of two opposites.
Your blood never was a discourse
Or a symbol to something that has taken place in past history.
Because you have poured your life into us
In order to pass over to us
And to remove all the boundaries of death, time and space.

Your infinite love cannot be a prisoner of such boundaries
Or be held captive to all the definitions that we have created.
You pass over them with such a unique compassion.
You do not care what we say about you
But you care about how we love you

Because you are eternal, always present in time
And you desire to dwell in all of us.

And time is smaller than a drop of rain in your hand.
You do not pass over from the past to the present
But the present passes over to you, the Eternal One.
Whenever we need life, we pass over to you
Because you want your blood to be active in us
And that our life will become your blood and your life.

What a great glory that you have united us with your self-giving
That we may truly become the cup of your immortal love
In this mortal life.
O Jesus, the Light of Life,
Glory be to you.

Psalm 55

Jesus is Our Love and Our Life

O Jesus, my Lord, you have received all of me with my infirmities
In order that I may receive all of you with your glory.

I come to you dirty
In order to become pure like you.

I receive all of you in order that I will sit next to you,
In order to sit in the glory of your divine throne
And inherit with you, your kingdom.

Your glory, O Jesus, is your love that does not change,
The divine sun that does not set in the horizon.
You truly are the resurrection
And I have known you as life, O Jesus.
The victorious over every obstacle,
You are my love and my life.

Psalm 56

Jesus, with You There is No Guilt or Shame

O Lord,
Is it our despair and our guilt that have created
Our sense of separation from you?

I cannot imagine
That after you became human
You could reject any human
Because this means you are rejecting yourself and your incarnation.

I cannot imagine
How you went through the lifecycle of humanity,
From birth to death.
Burial.
But the resurrection has confirmed your eternal union
With our humanity.

Why did you come back to our human life?
If you had rejected your humanity, you would not have
Raised our humanity from the grave
And we would not have been redeemed by you.

All sense of rejection and fear is the fruit of our death.
We imagine that you rejected us
And that sense of rejection is part of our self-defense
Because of our mortal being
And we think that it has the right to exist forever.
But all things around us come out of this earth
And return back to earth
And we eat of the earth in various forms
In bread and meat
And drink it in the form of wine.

You came to convert what is mortal to what is immortal,

Yet our mortality presses on us so hard
That we cannot see the immortal in you.

O Lord,
I was under the weight of my guilt for so many years
Until finally the light of your incarnation penetrated
The prison of my mortality.
Severed all the chains
And made me free.

For now I see myself in you, as you see yourself in me.
No moral quality is required
But only mutual love.
Not even faith that has been magnified by the church.
What a strange way of telling me I need to have faith –
It is almost like saying, "Try to be human."
My existence as human is my faith.
It is also my love,
And that goes back to you.

Glory be to you, Redeemer and King.

Psalm 57

Jesus, into Your Hands We Deliver Our Life

"Into your hands I deliver my spirit,"
The innocent cried out to you, Father
So that the guilty may cry out
"Into your hands," I put all of my being.

Into your hands that have accepted the Spirit of your Son.
I, too, deliver my spirit
Because of his hands that were nailed.
His will to die,
His love to give up his life.
I, too, not having the same pure hands
Nor the will to give up my life
Not to mention my very weak love.
But Jesus my Lord,
Being me, the very me
At your divine throne,
I dare to say, "Into your hands I deliver my life."

Psalm 58

Jesus – the Light of Our Darkness

Why do you, Lord, hide in the human heart?
Why do you keep revealing your glory to the last day?
You love us
Yet you want us to come to you freely,
Not over-powered by your glory,
Which can freeze our being.
For your glory surpasses all that we know about beauty or majesty.
They can actually kill us.
For your splendor is mightier than all that we know
Of the splendor of creation.

You like to hide, where, in the darkness of our heart, you seek rest.
For you had this darkness in your heart when you became human
But you changed it,
Made your humanity grow up,
Mature in union with the Father and the Holy Spirit.
Since then you have visited all of our darkness by your teaching
And by your death and resurrection, and by coming to dwell in us.
When you completed creating us in you
By changing our humanity in you,
Our darkness became a challenge for you.
So you continue to come to visit our humanity
And make it your dwelling.

Come and rest in the darkness of my heart
So that your light may give me life, and guide me
To the light of union with you.

Psalm 59

Jesus – the Light of Every Generation

Once a year we have a Holy Week and an Easter Day –
What a great error!
For you, Lord, love to be born in all of us
And to crucify our old life,
And to raise us with you.

Paul who had the once a year celebration of Passover
Opted out when he understood that you, Lord, are "our Passover."
He died "to the Law" to live the new life for you.

You, Lord, are not under the hegemony of times and seasons.
Not because you do not love time, not at all,
For you created time and seasons.
There is nothing human or for humans
Which you have created that you hate.
For there is no hatred in you, not even our wounds called sins,
Which are a challenge for you to heal.

O Lord of all times,
Where all times become seasons for revelation of the eternal,
Your plan is to visit time by making it
A witness to your redeeming love.
You do not drag the past to the present,
But your eternal love shines, and the past becomes present
Because you are the past and the present and the coming life.

Psalm 60

Jesus – Unique Love

Your love has changed everything.
Your love has its own values,
It has its own measure.
It is a model for itself.
Your love demands new words.
Our old words are like the old garment
And your love is the new patch.
You give life to sinners and this is where all of our values collapse.
You became what you are not: human.
And here there is no measure that can measure your self-emptying.
You are the model of your love,
For no one before you gave up his life for the unworthy.
Teach me this love,
Since all of our concepts of love are tarnished
By the rubbish of our feeble imagination.
For each concept we have is a by-product of our mortal life.

Psalm 61

Jesus – Giver of Life

O Jesus, your incarnation was not a step toward the cross.
You were crucified the day you were conceived by the virgin
Because in her womb you emptied yourself for our sake,
Becoming what you are not - a human.
The narrow space of the womb of the virgin
Became the boundaries in which you lived as an embryo.
You knew and you tasted the narrow space of our creation
Which is not different from the narrow tunnel of our death
Through which you travelled when you were crucified.

Your incarnation was a definition of your being.
You had a foretaste of it by conception and birth,
And manifested it on the cross, the most obvious self-emptying.
Your incarnation grew up like a tree
Bearing fruit of eternal giving.

You accepted death as you accepted birth.
You were not born in order to die,
But born in order to destroy death.
By your conception and birth
You have transformed the law of biology, the source of our death.
For every person born of a woman is born to die
But you are born for life.
"I am the life and the resurrection."
And you truly are the life and the resurrection
Because by life you come to revive us
And by resurrection you make our life immortal.

Psalm 62

Jesus – the Healer of Our Distorted Vision

Our songs dried up when you became a price given to the Father,
As if the Father needed a price while he is one with you.
He is in you, and you are in him.
How did you become a price for our sins?
The Father is your love and you are the child of his love.
How can love seek a price?
Love does not seek its own right.
If love seeks anything, it becomes law,
For law organizes and seeks the way of punishment.
But divine love gives, even to the unworthy.

You give up your life
And your sacrificial love is not according to the law.
Your courage to love sinners harnesses me
And puts a bit on my tongue
Because I am not free like you and cannot love like you.
I cannot cross over the boundaries,
While you crossed all boundaries when you became man.

O why has your incarnation not taught us
That there is no boundary you did not cross?
You took what is contrary and different from your own nature,
What is totally different from your person.
You became man, living our own weakness.
You did not sin, because you did not live for yourself.
Some of our sins are seeking the infinite
And the contradiction of sin is that a finite cannot become infinite.
But you, the infinite, united yourself to the finite
To show us, the finite, how to love infinitely like you.

But we left love alone.
We were seeking you in the commercial places,
Trying to find words and concepts to express your love.

Defiling your love with our human concepts.
Our law became understanding theology
And our imaginations became doctrines.
We imposed on you boundaries created by our minds,
Defined by our minds and by our language,
Which is the defense of our mental abilities
Coming from a dry source that has been subjected to mortality,
Unable to perceive self-giving as a true way of life.

But you, Lord, don't take notice of any of that.
You still shine with your love in the dark night of our thoughts.
How wonderful and glorious is your love,
O my Lord Jesus.

Psalm 63

Jesus – Our Spring of Life

O Lord Jesus, you are my God and my King.
You are the morning that brings the light of immortality.
The light of the day makes me long
For the Light of your resurrection.
You are life and without you I have no life in me.
You are hidden in my mortal being, like my heart in my chest.
You beat silently waiting for my return to you
When my daily life takes me away from you
And my awareness is no longer with you.
I thirst for you.
I hear what you said to the Samaritan woman:
The water that I give will flow for eternal life.
And since I have known you, you have become that water,
Giving life; not only to me, but to all.
You do not wait for our response, but you come to us
To put that response in our heart,
Or you wait until our thirst for you becomes a burden for our being
And thus we wake up from the slumber of our life.
O Jesus, you are the help that leads us to the true help.
Truly, Lord, without you we can do nothing.

Psalm 64

Jesus – Our Fountain of Eternal Life

Jesus my Lord,
My Daily Bread,
Light Eternal,
King of Love,
Savior of sinners,
Shine into our hearts.
Build your throne in our life,
Mediator and Intercessor,
Head of New Creation.
Your love is your blood,
Mingled with us mortals,
Washing away sins.
At your altar
We meet
To drink from the fountain
Of your eternal life.

Psalm 65

Jesus – Conqueror of Death

You were born in our time in order to contain time
Anointed as a king to captivate humanity by your love.

The Spirit of Holiness, who has comfort in you, anointed you.
And by resting in you, the Spirit has his own
Eternal comfort in humanity,
Becoming a gift for sinners.

You were crucified on the cross in order to contain death.
You contain death in order to abolish it.
When you contained time, time ceased to be a boundary,
Time of acceptance or time of rejection.
For you filled all time,
You are the fullness of all.
You contain death because it was the end
And the destruction of life.
And since you are life that cannot be destroyed,
From your cross shines the power of resurrection.
Death became like time — unable to stand
As an obstacle in your way.

On the cross you cried out loud, "It is finished" — a cry of victory.
Because all enemies, all obstacles, all forms of separations,
Death and life,
All were overpowered.
And the consolation of life has changed the cycle of our being.

Your cross planted a seed of life in the believers
And that seed became the tree of life that gave fruit to immortality.
O Jesus, born of the virgin by the Holy Spirit,
Our biological birth has ended by your birth.
And with it, our social ethnic origin has been wiped out.
O Jesus crucified in our flesh, your death destroyed

All of our values,
For there is no longer judgment according to values.

The sun of life is shining without an evening,
For you are that sun.
Glory be to you,
Light of light,
God of God.

Psalm 66

Jesus Changes Our Mortal Life to Heavenly Life

My life started with you.
Without you, I have no existence;
With you there is no end for my life,
Because you are my life's goal.
Time is not in you, but you are in time.
You are neither seasons nor ideas, for you are the Creator of time
And the illuminator of all rational life.
In you, there is no time for my beginning.
I have been born with you and in you, in the fount of baptism.
You are born with us because you have been born for us
And every member of your body you formulated
So that all members of your body the church
Will be made of your bones and your flesh.
Thus, I became like you - without beginning and without end.
You are the beginning that has no beginning,
And the end has changed and become a goal.
How great is your love, my Jesus!
For the old existence has been transformed
Only some shadows of it still linger.
They disappear in the light of the revelation of your love.
These shadows have no reality
But all that has been born of you is real.
O my Jesus,
You truly are the Alpha and the Omega that has no end.
Because the end is the bosom of the Father,
Where we all shall rest with you forever.

Psalm 67

Jesus – Purity of the Impure

O Jesus, I cry to you, my true existence.
The river of goodness, infinite love.
My life now and in the age to come.

Flowing with goodness,
You pour your life
In the most filthy, dirty being
In order to defeat evil in its own abode, which is the heart of man.
You washed the feet of the apostles, even the feet of Judas.
You are not frightened by our treachery,
Nor do you abhor the prostitutes.

The prostitute saw your purity and loved you
Because she saw in you what she had never seen in her clients.
She wept at your feet and washed them with her tears.
Your pure love had shaken her being
Like the trembling of an earthquake,
For you were the first one who did not want her body
Nor were you looking for a part of her flesh,
But were seeking the totality of her lost being.
She loosened the hair of her head and wiped off your feet.
For you were so unique that even the crown of her being
Had to become a towel for your dirty feet,
Which had carried the dust of the road.
So the crown of her head became under your feet
As if she was saying to you in her heart,
"I wish I could have seen you before.
I wish I would have known you, and encountered your fiery love."
Truly, my Jesus,
You touched what was left of the divine image in her
And that was enough to resurrect it from the filth
Into which she had sunk.

O Jesus, the purity of all the impure,
The shining light of all those who seek truth,
The pure love that meets our empty hearts,
Truly you are the cry of my being and its goal.

Psalm 68

Jesus Clothed Our Nakedness with Dignity

When I considered my being without you,
I found myself naked and empty,
Without hope, without life,
Having no meaning, having no purpose.

I read and studied too much,
And wandered in the labyrinth of books,
To and fro, left and right.
I came to a bottomless pit,
Like someone addicted to wine
Who cannot stop until he has drunk the whole bottle.
New ideas became my deadly addiction.

But in that darkness of my life, you revealed yourself.
When you shone, you gave me a meaning:
To become the son of the Father, like you.
To become free like you, that God may be
The cause of my existence.
The Father gave you to us so that we may become his children
And you give us back as your gift to the Father.
When I found a meaning of my life in your life,
My life became a spark of your life.
O Lover of Man, the dignity of man is with you and in you.

Psalm 69

Jesus – Union of God and Humanity

My past life, all of it, became nothing
When you became the origin of my existence.
You are the Creator who has woven my being.

When I tried to possess my being without you,
I was exiled into the land of misery
Until you came to me with the flood of your love.
I saw in you the perfect humanity that I was lacking:
Your divinity that transports your perfect humanity to me
And to the rest of mankind.

You completed my existence
By your conception, birth, and anointing at Jordan.
You perfected my existence on the cross,
When you destroyed death
And put an end to the tyranny of the grave.
The sun of your resurrection is shining with your love for man.
So it is that I find my being in you.

All past events, words and attributes,
Which people attach to you,
Which I once accepted and added to my being,
Those that I have known and those that I have desired,
All have vanished.

All definitions vanished when you came to reveal to me
The new existence.
I have no Father except your Father
And no womb gave me birth except the fount of baptism,
The place of our eternal birth.
My extended family has become all human beings.
The circle of fellowship has become so wide
It overcomes all traditions and the values of our time.

I became a friend, an intimate friend, of every human
In order to complete my new being, which is your being.
The distinction that evil brings to our life has vanished.
It has been replaced by another distinction, that of love.

O my being and my existence,
Jesus,
My new origin,
Who snatched me from the dust of the earth,
Who led me to a heavenly life.
O good compassionate Savior,
The whole of my being
Has been submerged in the sea of your grace.
My being became a testimony to your grace.
O Jesus the grace of the Father, shining always, with goodness
Glory be to you.

Psalm 70

Jesus Revealed Divine Love, Beyond Definition

O Jesus, all of the definitions in our mind cannot besiege you.
They may define your humanity
And may bring us close to your divinity,
But you will remain above all of our definitions,
Because you are God incarnate.

If we define you, all of our words are human
And so we define just one side of you.
While the other side, which is your divinity,
Remains above definition.
And the union of divinity and humanity
Is a mystery above every discourse.

As man, you are the only man in our history
Who did not live for himself.
You are the only one who is not under the law.
You loved your life, and gave it as an eternal gift.
Such love is unknown to us.

You destroyed the boundaries of death in order to come to us, alive
In order to live with us and in us.
O Jesus, your name transforms me to you.
From my selfish existence
To the distinction of communion which I have learned
From the union of the two natures in your person.
I loved your name so much that it became a song of my life.
The song that transports my being from a confused life
To the light of your love.

O Incarnate Love!
Your love was not an utterance
For it became incarnate in flesh and blood
In order to be divinized by your love.

Your flesh and your blood
It granted immortality because love does not die.
You are my love that cannot be separated from you.
But by you it gains strength
And defeats all forms of separation
Because it is the power of your resurrection
And the light of your divinity,
Which shines throughout all generations.

Psalm 71

Jesus, Discovered by Love

You are hidden and tucked within the creases of my being
So as not to obstruct my freedom,
As if you are a word that has not been uttered yet.
A sense that is lacking a word to give it flesh of expression
Like a picture about to be painted.
For you want from my will to accept this picture.
This is the shyness of your love and the respect of my being.

For you are not shy to call us your brothers
But the shyness of your love compels you not to interfere.
That is why you stand knocking at the door
Waiting for us to open the door of our perception.
Because you shed your love, a gift of free love
And your self-giving love is like a flood,
It starts like a drizzle of rain.

You do not lay a heavy burden on those who love you,
Asking us to shed our blood first.
You know that this is above our endurance,
We who are frightened of death.

O Jesus, my being, without you there is not anything
So I seek you in the fabric of my unknown deep existence.
Where you hide, waiting for me to discover you,
This constant discovery is the state of becoming.
But you lift up my vision to see your heavenly glory
So that when I see the end,
I pursue you to see you clearly in my heart
Where I sit on the throne of your divinity
Which is the end of every gift that has led me to such glory.

Psalm 72

Jesus, Unfading Light and Life

You established your eternal love by creating for us a universe.
Formed us according to your own image
That we may become like you.
As a gift, you gave us the cosmos and all that is in it
To learn how to grow up in our union with you,
To learn from creation your immense goodness
And to perceive your strength and your power
So as not to be afraid in times of tribulation.

Your name is above every name.
The flag of our salvation,
The light of the way of our life.
You have filled our being with your Spirit,
Transformed the earthly in us into heavenly.
What a great grace, that under my mortal skin,
Is the light of your divine life!
The first will fade away, but the second will be revealed.
The first Adam dies every day — natural death.
But you have removed the curse of death
In order that the new Adam may grow up.
And so, from the old and the dead, emerges new life.
What is old in us will fade away.
Not like the grass of the fields that becomes dry,
But as the darkness of night
Which is dispersed by the light of dawn.

O Light of our Life that does not set,
Glory be to you, because you have transformed us
From death to life!

Psalm 73

Jesus – in Us to Grow and to Mature

The union of your divinity with our humanity
Is the eternal shelter of all those who seek to be united with you.
As your humanity grew up in you,
So also my humanity will grow up in union with you.
You hear the beats of my heart
Because they are part of our incarnate life.

My salvation is marked by the destiny of your humanity,
That humanity which has been glorified
To stand up as a witness for our salvation,
To give us participation in the glory of your sonship.
Before I came to the womb of my mother, you were watching me,
Waiting for my birth, in order to reveal yourself.
So my days became your days.
We live them together, in order that my body may mature
And my soul may grow up in the knowledge of your love.
You teach me the mystery of my union with you
So that I may proclaim this mystery to the coming generations.
That your mercy is forever,
O Holy One of the Church.

Gather us together in the mystery of your love
So that the Father and the Holy Spirit may be revealed
By you in us.

Hallelujah.

Psalm 74

Jesus is the End of Fear and Death

My Lord Jesus,
You have planted the power of your cross in our decaying history.
You have transformed our suffering and pain
Into a means of progress.
You have accepted death in order that
Life may not be subjected to fear.
The evil are proud of their power,
They trample the weak under their feet with joy.
Thus, I see Calvary existing in every street in every city.
The crucified and the crucifier are every day on every page
Of our newspapers.

But with you, Lord, the cross was not an end, but a beginning.
From the cross we learn that the annihilation of the weak is the end of power.
For power that defeats, and tramples all under its feet,
At the end will destroy even itself.
The blood of our human martyrs
Has created history for many nations,
And from this blood a new life has emerged.
The fear of individuals does not create history.
But the solidarity of the weak can defeat tyranny.

You are with us and in us as a living one crucified.
You are alive and we are, by you, alive.
And the wounds of your cross are chapters of our age,
But the end of these chapters are known to you and to us.
It is the resurrection, your resurrection and our resurrection.
For you are our life that cannot be separated from you,
O One who defeated death and crucified fear.
You start to write, with your cross,
The same history in each one of us.

Psalm 75

Jesus is Eternally Divine and Human for Humanity

Whenever I see a cross,
I bow down to you
In my heart.
I catch the sight of your sacrificial love.

I touch any cross I see
For it is our bond of love.
You have tied your feet with those nails.
You revealed your hands and your side to Thomas,
But not your feet
For they are fixed by your love to keep you forever as the Savior.

The name you took when Mary conceived you
Is an everlasting name.
Because you will be the Savior always, even in the next life.
For we need your lordship to know how to live eternally like you.

O my Lord, from eternity you came
To take us through our history to eternity.
And there we need you to cleanse us
From what we have learned from our earthly life.
Jesus, my eternal love
In you,
Love and life merge and become one.

Psalm 76

Jesus is Born Every Moment into Human Filth

My Love, when I hear the songs of what we call Christmas,
My heart aches for you.
For we go shopping and eating - what we call Christmas.
Food of a different kind.
But you were born in a filthy and dirty place
And we make it clean and shining
By means of our plastic dolls
And clean mangers.

O my Love,
You will come to our human hearts
Which are dirtier than the stable.
Not the natural dirt of fodder and animal droppings,
But all of the horrible vices of our humanity
Which are totally alien to proper humanity.
There is the demonic hatred that brings other vices.
And you my Love must clean all of that
Murder and abnormal behavior.
O what a deception to live the fancy side of the story of Christmas
And to forget the dirty part.

Now, Lord, here is my dirty heart, where your love is just a guest.
Here is where I give you just a small corner
So I can eat my Christmas food
And push away the reality
Of how you took what is totally different from your divine life.
Only you can live a life that is totally alien and opposite
Of what you are in reality.

Psalm 77

Jesus is Revealed to Share His Life

Today they told us that it is marked in the calendar as Good Friday,
The day of your self-giving which we call death.
My Lord, no one can give up his or her life without dying
And, O my Savior, I have just begun to understand how Paul said
That he was crucified with you.
One must die to have a taste of your sacrificial love,
And to die to myself will make every day my Good Friday.
When you and I are brought to the altar of love,
You will drive your love like a knife to split my being
And to take away all that is of value according to the world
And create a new life that has its center in you.
I will make the sign of the cross.
It is like the knife of your love.
It cuts off all the values that have been established in our world,
Those that have shaped the life I have lived without you.

Psalm 78

Jesus – Our Purification and Freedom

Your name is the antidote for many things,
But above all for our impersonal love,
A product of our fallen nature,
When we change living persons to concepts and to ideas.
In my exile in the desert of so-called theology,
You, my Love, became a course that I used to teach
Called Christology.
But your Name forced me back to your Person.
To the glory of your Mystery that cannot be defined by any idea,
I will cling to your name lest I go back to my illness
Where persons become numbers or titles
And are reduced to concepts.
O my Love, impersonal love is our self-reflection
Of our inability to love persons,
Where equality and freedom demands commitment to persons.

Psalm 79

Jesus Unmasked Our Humanity

Clothes, work, education, and many other things
Made me an actor,
A man of a manufactured ID.
I acquired multiple images when I performed,
All of them are functional and they eat up my inner life
Where I live on the verge of a reality that I have created for myself.
Come and save me, Lord Jesus, from this very artificial life,
From all the masks that are required by our social life
And destroy our love.

You emptied yourself when you poured out your life
Into the form of a slave who has no social or political affiliation.
We made your self-emptying a chapter in books,
Called it "kenosis" and debated it.
O my Lord, you did not live for yourself.
If you did, your death would have been involuntary.
But freely you gave up your life
And so it is that you forgave those who crucified you,
For they helped you to do what you came to do.
Taking the form of a slave made you free from all needs.
You even stripped your divine life of its glory and power.
You had no need to live according to divine glory and power

O, now I know that you gave up perfection
To be the Head of the non-perfect
Changing the movement of holiness itself,
For you died by hanging even holiness itself.
You gave up your lordship and became a slave,
Which is beyond my understanding.
For no one who is divine can taste death, even in his flesh.
You did not put on our humanity as a mask,
But you put on humanity for your life eternal
And this is the meaning of your resurrection.

Help me love you, and become like you.
For this is the only way to be a real human.

Psalm 80

A Psalm for Jesus, My Brother

Have mercy, Lord Jesus, for I am your brother.
It is hard for so many of us to call you our brother.
But in calling you my brother, I also confess your divinity.
No one can become the loving brother of the whole human race
Throughout human history, except you.
You love us without reason.
Your love for our fallen humanity is what made you become man.
My brother, here I am.
You who shared with me my humanity,
Which was and is your free choice,
To assure me of the truth of your love.
In you, Jesus, not only love and life are one
But also divinity and humanity are one.
They are united forever
To make divine love human
And human love divine.

Psalm 81

Jesus – Our True Union with the Father

Your love and life are one.

You have freely allowed others to take part of you.
The sick.
The naked.
The prisoner and the hungry.
You are in all of these
Because in love you unite yourself with your beloveds.
It is true and real unity.

My Lord, you are in me and with me
And as I seek to be like you, you help me to be as such.
Yet at the same time, you help me to keep my uniqueness
Even though my uniqueness has been damaged by my sins.

To be unique in you and with you
Does not make me an identical copy of you,
For your love is not narcissistic.
You see, in each one of us, his or her needs as your needs,
Those of the fallen and those who are struggling just to be human.

O Lord, you are far from being a universal man
Or even the ideal man.
You are the man for men, males and females.
We assign a gender for you
To keep you out of your infinite love for humanity.
We made you male because we saw in you our maleness.
But you, Lord, are the Savior of both males and females.
To restore life to a male is to make him human
And it is the same for a female.
Love transcends gender when it is sacrificial love,
But it can be gender motivated if it is only for self-satisfaction.
Save me Lord from all classifications

Lest I become a pagan who worships himself
In the closed circle of the vision of the ego.
Be my supreme ego
Who lives and loves just like you.

Psalm 82

Jesus – the Deification of Love

My church cast me out because of my writing
And teaching on deification.
Deification in you and by you.
Your shame has reached me.
You wanted me to have a little taste of your rejection.
My friends still fight me on our participation
In the "divine nature."
O my Love, your love is both divine and human
But is one Love of the one Lord and the one Savior.
We are afraid of the divine but we are also afraid of the human
And therefore, union is a problem for us.
Union is what we cannot accept, but division is what we love.
We find our ego in our divisions and we love them
Because we are afraid to give up what we like and what we love.
True deification is the fruit of your love.
We cannot achieve it or have it from any other source,
Only from your union with us.

How is it that you are the Head of the new humanity
Called your Body,
Or called by another name, the Church?
How can you be in us and with us and for us
By only a human link, such as solidarity?
How can our solidarity become eternal?
Your incarnation is the foundation of the Church,
Giving the Church the very name of your life
In the flesh, your Body.

O my Lord and my Love,
Will you give your very self to me in the Mystical Supper
And then say, "Take, eat, this is my body - but
Don't come near my divinity"?
No. Rather you say, "Drink this cup, which is my life,"

For blood and life are the same.

For 2,000 years we have been eating your body
And drinking your blood,
But both of them have never come to an end.
The miserable talks about this Supper are too painful to repeat
Because in all of the debates we were never able
To see that your Mystical Supper is the Gift of Love.

O Lord, I receive you for my body
And I receive you for my spirit
Because you see my body and my spirit as your own inheritance
And because you have the same humanity,
Yet glorified by the victory over mortality,
Which is the cause of death.
If your divinity does not dwell in me to change me to your glory,
How can I truly love your divine person –
And reject your humanity?
For the word "half" is a word of division
And you came to destroy our divisions.

Save me, my Brother, from false teachers.

Psalm 83

Jesus – Our Dwelling in the Love of the Father

Today you have baptized me
And also in you I was baptized in that old church in old Cairo.
Baptism never left me, for it captured me
And it is always within me when I make the sign of the cross
Or call you my Lord.
It was the beginning of your constant washing of all of my filth
And the beginning of revealing yourself and leading me
To the Father.
Truly you made me one with you by this grace of baptism
And truly I was born with open eyes
To see the great gift of adoption.

I am your brother by adoption.
This is the greatest gift:
To be called from this biological life,
To be transformed to the divine life,
And to rest with you in the "bosom" of the Father.

O Lord, those who died before your restoration of
Humanity to full communion with your Father by the Holy Spirit,
These rested in the "bosom" of Abraham.
But now this is no longer the case
For all of us are resting with you in the "bosom" of the Father.
The "bosom" of the Father is not a place;
It is the intimate love
Which you have made available for us by your incarnation.
Now a human is in the Godhead –
What a change for the nature of the slaves
Who are now liberated from the laws of the earthly life
And partake of the life that has no subjection to laws,
Any laws.

Psalm 84

Jesus – Our Prayer to the Father in the Holy Spirit

Jesus pray in us the prayer which you want to utter.

Jesus pray with us the prayer which you long to hear.

Jesus pray for us for we do not know what we have to say.

Jesus pray in us the same prayer you said when you were baptized.

Jesus pray in us the same prayer when you broke the bread
In the upper room.

Jesus pray for us to receive from you the whole sum of the
Prayers of your Father and of your Spirit

Jesus pray in us the same prayer which you said
When you were on the cross.

Jesus pray with us the very words when you were washing the
Feet of the apostles and when Judas kissed you.

Jesus pray for us to know what you used to say to the
Father every morning.

Father pray in us the same unutterable prayer which
You prayed when your Son was begotten before all creation.

Father pray with us the same prayer you prayed when
You sent your Son into the world.

Father pray for us when we cannot understand your Son and
We stumble over his humanity.

Father pray in us the same words which you said when

You baptized your Son and anointed him with your Spirit.

Father pray with us the same unutterable prayer which
You prayed when your Son died on the cross.

Father pray for us to hear the same cry which you say when
You hear the Spirit and the Son cry "Abba Father."

Spirit pray in us the prayers which you taught the incarnate Son.

Spirit pray with us the true intercessions of your love.

Spirit pray for us to be the true image of your love.

Spirit pray in us the same unutterable prayer which
You prayed when you saw your companion become human.

Spirit pray with us the same prayer which you uttered at Pentecost.

Spirit pray for us that we become your prayer.

Jesus pray for us to be one with you in the
Unity which is above every unity.

Father pray in us the same prayer which
You share with the Son and the Spirit.

Spirit pray with us the same prayer with which you inspired
Jesus to reveal to us the unutterable unity of the Godhead.

Jesus pray in us the prayer which you want to utter in us that
We may become one with you.

Jesus pray with us the prayer which you long to hear when
We forgive others as you did.

Jesus pray for us, for we do not know how to intercede and
How our intercession becomes the fire of your love.

Jesus pray in us the same prayer which you said when
You were baptized and accepted the Holy Spirit to
Preserve him in your person for us.

Jesus pray in us the same prayer when you broke that bread
In the upper room and give us the same longing to
Give up our life for you.

Jesus pray in us the same prayer which you said when
You were on the cross, the same seven words which
Opened Paradise to the thief.

Jesus pray with us the very words you spoke when
You were washing the feet of the apostles and
When Judas kissed you.

Jesus pray for us to receive from you the whole sum of the
Prayers of your Father and of your Spirit.

Psalm 85

Jesus, Our Hearts Are Your Favorite Dwelling Place

Come to my heart, Lord Jesus.
It is your favorite place,
Sinful as it was,
Sinful as it is.
But because of your love for sinners,
You gave your life.

That same steadfast love
Draws you to your favorite place.
On the cross you remembered the thief
To show us that in your suffering,
You foresaw all of us.
When all were remembered,
You cried out in a loud voice
"It is finished."

Psalm 86

Jesus is Our Eternal Bond

Here is heaven
And the angels.
All the saints.
Rejoice in us,
You my Lord.
Interceding but
Not with words.
Your love
Pours your life
To gather us
Into the Godhead.

Eternal Covenant
Gathering us,
Binding us forever.
Not life
Nor death,
Not sickness
Nor any loss
Can hinder us
From your redeeming love.

As the Good Shepherd,
You seek us.
Defending and guiding
Feeding us with your life
Enthroning us on your throne,
Your crown of righteousness.

Freely you give
To secure our acceptance
With all sinners.
Your glory

You have given
To unite us with your Father.

Your anointing
You have given
So the Spirit becomes our inheritance.
Glory be to the Father
Who sent you.
Glory be to the Spirit
Who,
For us,
Anointed you.

Psalm 87

Jesus – the Hope of the Fallen

My eternal foundation
Is in your incarnate person.
You love humanity more than all the glory of creation.

You did not share with any other creature the
Glory of your sonship.
Only with us humans.

O Son of Man,
And Son of God the Father,
You came to us incarnate.

Love is not an utterance.
It is life that uplifts the fallen
And revives the dead with eternal life.

Psalm 88

Jesus is Our Glory

My prayer to you, Lord Jesus, is your very words,
Even an echo of your voice.
It is not any longer my words, but yours, because we have one life.
Reciting your words is reciting what you have in your heart
Because you see with our eyes what we see
And you feel what we feel.
But boredom does not besiege you.
That is why you come to liberate us from our boredom
By your Sweet presence.
You are not defeated by temptations.
That is why you come to defeat ours.

O mighty fighter!
The conqueror of hell,
The destroyer of death and the victor over Satan.
You hanged judgment on the cross.
You scattered all our fanciful ideas about God by the
Light of your love.
Grant me what you have, that our union may be perfect.
Glory be to you, my master and my king.

When you created us, you had prepared a place for us,
In you, by your incarnation.
You gathered up all of our days like little drops of water in the
Mighty palm of your hand.
You made our eternal rest in you
And you call us to come to you to be united to you.

When you became human, you were counting all your lovers
Calling them to the banquet of your love
To plant the gift of your sonship in each one of them.
By grace you have liberated us from the slavery of our nature,
And by you we have been lifted up

To the glory of our union with you.
By your incarnation you have established our being in you and
In the Godhead,
And so you have made us your eternal inheritance.

O Lover of Man, our ages are pages in your plan.
On each page you write multiple verses of your mercy.

Psalm 89

Jesus – Confirmation of the Covenant of Divine Love

There is no love greater than your love.
I shall sing your love with all your lovers –
The saints, the martyrs, and all of those who passed into the
Bath of repentance.

You established the covenant of your love by your incarnation
And confirmed that covenant when you abolished death.

Your love for humanity gave us immortal life by your resurrection
In order that your love may become immortal in us.

You granted us immortal love
To enjoy your love and to be seated
On your divine throne in heaven.

For you do not desire that this throne will be yours alone.
You are generous and good,
Full of goodness that keeps nothing to yourself
Including your eternal glory.

Psalm 90

Jesus – the Fire of the Eternal Flame of Love

O Lord Jesus, you are with us
And if we leave you, you seek us.
Before you created heaven and earth,
You saw each one of us,
Watching the hearts in which you would be coming to live.
In your eternal abode in heaven
You looked down and saw in the life of the most miserable sinner
A potential child that will inherit the eternal kingdom.
With your tender mercy, you lead us to your glory
And with your love, you inspire us to seek you.
Calling us secretly by that deep longing
Which is diverted to multiple goals
And adds thirst and emptiness together to us.

But you, Lord, in your mercy,
Wait till we are fed up with our mortal life.
You come to rescue us from our state of boredom
And to lift us up from the pit of the darkness of life
Where there is no hope
And give us hope in a new life which you share with us.

Come, Lord Jesus,
For my hunger cannot be satisfied with anything I have.
It is only satisfied with your presence
Which makes me forget even my existence.
I become one with you.
There is no longer me or you,
But us.

Psalm 91

Jesus – the Dwelling of the Triune Love

He who dwells in love of the Triune God
Has a taste of eternal life
And shall abide with Christ Jesus forever, in the Father
And the Holy Spirit.

My Lord Father who loves us
And gave his Son as a Gift of Life for us,
We call on you in Jesus
To open our vision to see the Triune divine communion of love.
Deliver us from the snare of division
That blinds us from seeing your love
And from the deadly pestilence of hatred.

Send your Holy Spirit to give us a share in your life
That all evil powers may be set to naught.
Remember us Father,
That we are the members of the body of your Son
Who saved us from eternal damnation.

The heavenly powers see us in your Son
And when they sing to him, we are adored by them
Because by your incarnation, Lord Jesus,
You are our dwelling-place in the Godhead.

Your faithful love is our shield
And your mediation, Lord Jesus,
Is our eternal hope.
You keep us as the vine keeps its branches and leaves
And you nourish us with the sap of your life-giving presence.
Halleluiah.

Psalm 92

Jesus – Divine Touch of Life and Hope

The morning light brings to our awareness the
Light of your resurrection
And so we sing to your everlasting love of our humanity.
At mid-day your death for us is the
Eternal covenant of your faithfulness.
The setting of the sun,
The curtain of the night,
Calls us to rest under the power of your protection.
I stretch my hands
As you did on the cross
To make peace, to rejoice in your reconciliation.

Everything around us
Is like the finger-print of your plan of salvation.
The seasons and death
Growing of all that die in winter
Speak to us of the coming glory
Of your Day
When you come to restore life to the dead.
The air is a spark of the Breath of Life,
The same that you breathed on the apostles in the upper room.
The fruits of the earth,
Which are sweet and beautiful,
Speak of the fruits of the Spirit
As sweetness of heavenly life.

Everything has a print of you.
How marvelous are you,
My Lord Jesus.

Psalm 93

Jesus – Breath of Love

Each breath is a song of your love.
It comes from his gift,
From your life.
Every warmth comes from the heat of your love,
From you my Lord Jesus.

My heart receives your love, surprised by grace.
It has the fragrance of your Spirit.
The smell of Jordan.
The sweat of Gethsemane.
It is you, Jesus.

Your blood of your cross
Is in me.
Your blood makes me like you.
When together we kiss an enemy,
Your blood in my being gives me our common life.
Your name is the constant divine kiss
Which we can share with everyone.

Psalm 94

Jesus – a Song for the Lover of My Soul

We read together the Song of Songs to the end.

He danced and said, "I shall show you the greatest Song of Songs."

No lover ever gave his body as food.
No lover poured his blood from heart to heart and stayed alive.
In love, you and I both live the cross.
The resurrection made the cross my way of life.
So you and I live together,
Pass together the gates of death.

Come let us drink.
Tonight we shall celebrate
My love for sinners.
Let us eat the bread
Which I have baked
Through the fire of my love.

Tonight we shall sit in the upper room.
I shall feed you with my life
Till you become like me.

When you as a sinner sit on my throne,
I will know then that I am not on my own.
Only then my pain and yours will come to an end.
The songs of the angels are sweet,
Your simple words are the best.
Your words of prayer are more precious than all heaven.

Your tears of longing bring what happened in Bethlehem
When I Left my glory for you.
Your pain is like the nails,
Like the darkness of hell,

Where I was looking for your heart,
Lost in the flood of despair

Wait for me my beloved.
I have waited for years to rescue you.
Wait, for my love will never expire.
I seek you as the fruit of my love.

Jesus, come and give a kiss.
His kiss is a word,
His word is his lips,
His lips are his promise,
His promise is his person.

Your heart utters words.
Do not say to me, "I love you."
I hear this from all sinners.
But when you say, "I am you,"
Only then will my heart rest.
When you will be me, I will be you.

Psalm 95

Jesus – Immortal Joy of Our Humanity

You came to tell us that you are the resurrection and eternal life.
These words were fulfilled in you,
By your union with our humanity, your death and resurrection.

You do not suffer death only once,
For when we die with you in the mystery of baptism
Our death is eliminated by your death on the cross.
Your death gives life.

We are crucified with you in order that we may
Celebrate your sacrificial love
By which you have destroyed all forms of separation.
You did not come back to life, as if you had been resuscitated,
But you were raised up by the power of the Spirit
To unite the Spirit to your plan of salvation and
Receive the same life
That you have received from the Father.

Save me, Crucified Jesus,
From the fear of the slaves
Who imagine that their immortality is in the flesh,
While time and illness and its growing old
Tell us that our flesh is not our eternal abode.

I wonder at your great sacrificial love in which you give us
Your body and your blood.
You deliver your life to us in order to taste the power of giving up,
And by receiving your body and your blood
You teach us the greatest revelation of love.
Love does not keep anything for itself;
It gives up in order that it may spread,
And your love has given us an extension of your life.
So we have become your life, and your resurrection,

And your witness in the world
Glory be to you.

Psalm 96

I - Jesus Crucified and Risen for Us

Blessed are those who draw the water of their love from the spring of the Crucified and graft the cross into their heart as the source of new life.

Happy are those who treasure the love of the Crucified in their heart; they will always find peace, for with the cross there is eternal peace of reconciliation.

To walk with the Crucified daily is to abandon the values of the world in order to harvest from the richness of his love, when he comes to share his glory with those who love him.

You called us to take our cross and to follow you to learn your sacrificial love. It is the love that will give us a place on your throne on the last Day of Judgment. You have given this command to teach us the eternal revelation of your love. If we fail to accept it, we fail to be partakers of your divinity.

Following you, carrying my cross – when I take this commandment and keep it, I am firmly establishing my being in your love.

I will thank you as I learn your saving judgment that you have declared by your cross. You judged us sinners to be made free from damnation.

I will keep your cross in my heart and will not utterly forsake your cross, but I will drink from the eternal spring of your love.

What is the true and sure way of life? It is holding fast to your cross, the path that you have opened and keep open for us, which is the full communion with your Father by the gift of your Spirit.

With my whole heart I have desired to be a bearer of my cross; in order not to lose the vision of your love.

If your cross is in my heart, I should not sin against you or against others, for we carry together the same fire of love.

II - The Divine Triumph

Blessed be you, O Lord, for you have revealed to us the sacrificial life that is marked by your cross. It is the eternal Tablet on which you recorded, with your blood, the triumph of love over hatred, of life over death, and where you wrote the forgiveness of sins and the abolishment of condemnation forever.

With my lips I praise your triumph on the cross as the divine triumph over all of our human concepts, for the power of your love has replaced the judgment of the old law.

The way of your cross is the melody of our praise, which is beyond all manner of all forms of speech.

I meditate on your cross. When I begin to look for a reason for your love, I stumble; but the path of your love is far above our understanding.

III - Your Cross is Your Kiss for Sinners

My delight shall be in your cross and I will not forget that this is the kiss of your love for us sinners.

You are gracious to your servant that you allowed me to be crucified with you, and so I participate in your revelation of love in my heart.

Open my eyes that I may see the wonders of the fountain of your love, which opened the gates of life to the thief; what wonderful love to save the worthless!

I am a stranger upon the earth; give me your strength that your love may be always like fire in me.

My soul is consumed with longing, since the fire of your love has changed my understanding of your judgments.

IV - Your Love is My Meditation

You have rebuked the arrogant by forgiving the prostitute and by blessing the poor; give me grace so I do not stray from your kingdom.

Remove from me the reproach and scorn of sinners, for I have accepted that you died to save sinners, among whom I am the first.

Loving sinners as you love them is very costly. This counsel is the meditation of your servant. It is the heart of your cross--the first step is to refuse to take part in any condemnation of sinners, because I am one among them.

I have recounted my ways and you have answered me from your cross in teaching me your statutes of your eternal forgiveness and love.

V - Your Love is Wonderful

Help me discern the way of your love, and I shall meditate on this wonder, for you never cast out sinners who come to you.

My soul melts away in the tears of my sorrow, my pride hides your love from me; raise me up because of your love and your humility that I may be glorified with you.

Take from me the way of falsehood, because you are gracious and do not condemn my weakness; for your crucified love is the spring of assurance of all sinners.

Lord, I am not ashamed of your wonderful love or of its mark, your cross.

VI - Freedom from Sin, Condemnation and Hell

You have opened for me the way of true freedom from sin, condemnation and hell. You have set my heart at liberty from fears; re-create me according to your love.

Teach me, Lord, the way of your love, and I shall keep it to the end. Give me understanding that I may keep your cross in my judgment, and I shall treasure its victory and joy in loving sinners in my heart.

Help me to walk in the path of your love, for in that way will I find my everlasting delight.

Make my heart incline to the judgment of your love, rather than to fame and to the love of power.

VII - You Alone Are My Life

Turn my eyes from gazing on worthless things, vainglory and temporary wealth; your way alone is the way of life.

On your cross you have confirmed to your servant your promise, which you have given for those who do not fear to be crucified with you.

Remove and take away every form of reproach because this I dread: whatever is not according to your love, is hell to me.

The only way to be one with you is to be crucified with you.

Your faithful love calls me to come. O Lord, your salvation is according to your judgment, which is to give life to all sinners.

I shall not answer those who taunt me with their judgment, for I have trusted in your judgment written with your blood on the cross. It is the judgment that gives life to the dead.

I am not ashamed of the revelation of your truth, the utterance heard from your lips, "Father forgive them." My hope is in this judgment. I shall always keep this love, now and forevermore. It is new and at the same time it is eternal, hidden from us. No one can reveal it but you, Eternal One.

VIII - Your Love is Freedom

I shall walk in the wide range of your freedom, for I have sought your teaching, which restored me to the freedom of a son.

I shall speak of your cross, even before the lovers of power. I will not be ashamed, for there is no shame in love.

My delight shall be always in your cross, it is the foundation of our common life and love.

My joy is to lift my hands up in praise of your redeeming love. It is the course of my meditation and the song of your faithfulness.

I remember your word on the cross to the thief and this gives me hope and burns the thorns of my doubts. Your promise to the one who stole paradise delights my heart.

The arrogant have refused to accept your love for sinners, but I have seen the miracles of your love in their life.

Lord, whenever I remember your crucified love, my comfort cannot be shaken.

I am seized with horror at the lack of mercy among some of those who believe in you, for they have forsaken your crucified love.

Your love has become melodies for me, my songs in the house of my pilgrimage. Your love shines in this dark world and those who seek your love will never miss it.

IX - Your Name Unites Me to You

I have recited your name in the night, O Lord, and this has kept the fire of your love present in my heart. I am strengthened by your name and your cross.

Your name, Lord Jesus, brings your cross. Neither can be separated from the other.

Lord, you are my portion; your love is the guarantee that you will seat me at your right hand on your throne on the Day of Judgment.

With all my heart I entreat you; keep me crucified with you that I may share in the glory of your resurrection.

X - Bridegroom of My Soul

I have considered my ways, and turned back from all that is alien to your love. I have made haste and not delayed in keeping your cross in my heart so that the world may be crucified to me, and I may be crucified to the world.

The wicked prepared their cords to wrap around me, but your cross cut them off and saved me from their snare.

At midnight I arise to celebrate your coming as the Bridegroom of my soul. With the sign of our wedding, the sign of the cross, I sign my being in order to enter the banquet of your love. So I become a companion to all those who are invited to this banquet; your cross is its only gate.

XI - How Can I Love like You?

Lord, heaven and earth are filled with your faithful love; I pray to you, teach me: How do you love each one of us?

You will deal kindly with your servant, in accordance with your crucified love. O Lord, Hell creeps on me whenever I remember my sins, but you have vanquished Hell.

Teach me true understanding and knowledge of your love lest I forget that it is the gift of your eternal kingdom.

I suffered when I went astray; your love leaves no room in my heart for any other alien love, but my assertive self-love troubles me and hinders me from loving you with total freedom.

You are kind and gracious; I pray you, teach me the freedom of your love.

The proud have smeared your cross with lies; the hardness of their heart is their law of death.

The heart of those who reject your cross is gross, saturated with the love of power; let me delight in the weakness of your love.

XII - Your Cross is Most Dear to Me

When I was afflicted, I was distressed. But contemplating your death, I learned your love that put an end to all forms of separation.

Most dear to me is your cross, the mark of your love; it is dearer than gold or silver--for these will perish, but your love is forever.

Your hands have made me and fashioned me; the same hands were nailed for my sake in order to give me an understanding of your love as my Creator, and also as my Redeemer.

Those who believe in you as their Creator must wait to hear the good news that you are also their Savior.

XIII - Jesus My Good Shepherd

I know, Lord, that your love is true, and your faithfulness will allow me to be united with you, especially in my troubles.

May your faithful love comfort me when I go astray; as a Good Shepherd you will not abandon me, a lost sheep.

May those who fear you know that losing your love is worse than Hell.

Let my heart be whole in your love, that I may not be put to shame when I face you on the Day of Judgment.

My soul longs for the discovery of the depth of your love and I hope that when this happens, fear will not devour me.

My heart is watching for the revelation of the depth of your love for this is the goal of my life.

XIV - Your Patient Love Guides Me

Lord, you have waited for years for me to come to you, this is your faithful love that knows how to wait, for you are always patient.

How many are the days of your servant; any one of them which has no spark of your love I count as if I am in the grave.

The proud have dug pits of hate in which to bury their enemies. They have not understood that you crucified hatred on Calvary and buried it in the grave.

Lord Jesus, your love is true; help me to cope with those who insist on subjecting your love to reason.

The proud count their success without any attention to love and forgiveness; thus being far away from your cross, their success destroys their love because it becomes their goal.

You give me life every day according to your faithful love, so I keep the testimonies of your cross.

Everlasting is your love, O Lord; it stands forever in the heavens, and takes delight in our humanity.

Your faithfulness remains through all generations – you have established it. For heaven and earth will pass away, but your crucified love will remain forever.

XV - Your Cross and Your Resurrection Are Your Victory

You have stored your resurrection in your cross, and life stands firm at the center of your love. Life has the royal seal of your blood.

If your Crucified love had not been my delight, I would have perished because of my weaknesses. Do not allow me to love you less than you love me.

I will never forget your love, for it is only because of your love have you given me life.

I am yours for you have purchased me with your blood; I will be in your presence as your inheritance, even if my love grows cold.

When the wicked wait for me in order to destroy me, it is time to embrace your cross.

I have seen an end of all things, but your love has no end or limits.

XVI - Your Cross is Special Wisdom

Lord, it is your love that teaches me how to love. All day long it is my meditation.

The wisdom of your cross makes me wiser than all; by this I can see that good triumphs at the end.

My teachers who embraced your love have gained wisdom, for love is the true school of the highest wisdom.

I have gained understanding that there is a particular knowledge in love. It gives birth to hope and faith.

XVII - Your Call is Always Sweet

From every evil path I hold back my feet, so that I may not become blinded by my sin, leading to the dark end of evil.

I have not turned aside from your love, for you have become my teacher and your cross has become the seal of the truth of your teaching.

How sweet is your call to me to come to you; it is sweeter to my ear than honey to my tongue.

From your cross I received the understanding of the nature of the power of love; therefore, I learned to reject all forms of love that do not have the cross at the center.

Psalm 97

I - Your Cross is a Lantern to My Life

Your cross is a lantern to my life; the light of your love enlightens my path.

I have tied my life to your cross and you will fulfill your promise to show me the glory of the resurrection.

I am greatly afflicted when I abandon your love; Lord, I lose my way and become alien to my true self.

Your love revealed your utter humility to accept my life as a sacrifice. This little offering is more precious in your sight than heaven.

My life is ever on the palm of your hand; it rests on the mark of your cross.

The wicked have set a snare for me – they scorn my life as an offering. This is just a drop of your suffering.

You have put your cross as a mark on every offering. You gave me confidence to claim your life as the altar for my sacrifice.

II - Your Cross Put an End to My Old Way of Life

I have inclined my heart to fulfill your call always, even to the end. Your cross is the only end, hidden from the beginning.

To keep my life for myself makes me double-minded. It is the way to perdition. Love without self-denial is the mark of Hell.

You are my hiding-place and your cross is my shield. It shields me from false love.

Away from me, all my lusts, that I may keep the fire of the love of my crucified God. For the end of every lust is the loss of love.

Sustain me according to your promise, that I may live crucified; let me not depart from this unique love.

Hold me and I shall be saved from seeking another love; keep me that I may ever gaze upon your cross and learn this eternal truth.

Those who reject your love go astray from their real self, and from you, and deceive themselves when they seek salvation without the cross.

All the wickedness of the earth is caused by the absence of love; but true goodness is in keeping the Law of your Love.

III - I Can Not Love You by My Strength Alone

My flesh trembles, waiting for the outpouring of your Spirit of Love; by my strength alone I cannot love you.

Without your love there is nothing acceptable to you. Without love, I may slip into the pit of hate. Your cross points to the pit of hate, which maximizes self-interest. This is the arrogant attitude which ends in distraction.

If my eyes fail to see the path of your salvation, deliver me by your redeeming love and grant me the vision of your glory.

By nature I am your servant, but by grace you granted me the gift of adoption. I bind myself to the cross of your Son so to enter into the fullness of your grace.

When your cross is despised, O Lord, it is time to witness, for there is no shame in love.

IV - Your Love Has its Law; to Give to the Unworthy

Truly by the Law of your Love, I have learned love; therefore I adhere to all of your commandments more than to my life itself.

I hold dear your cross which illuminates all your precepts; this protects me from falsehood, and I utterly abhor what is not from true love.

Your witnesses are wonderful, they are sealed by your blood. Your love for humanity is proven by your incarnation. Your sacrifice has opened the door of the kingdom to the unworthy. And as for your resurrection – it has sealed all with the seal of immortality and incorruption.

You opened the Scriptures to give me light; you gave me the Holy Spirit to discover the Scriptures and to learn wisdom.

I open my mouth to receive your Breath of Life that I may live according to the Law of your Love.

How gracious are you Lord Jesus to me; according to the judgment of your love I am a coheir with you.

Order every day of our life together by your word, that I may live in union with you.

Redeem me from man's cruelty, that I may keep your precepts and not imitate the cruel who do not know your cross.

Cause your face to shine upon your servant, and teach me to know the wisdom of your love.

V - My Love is Weak

My tears run down with rivers of water, because the more I long to be crucified the more I realize the weakness of my love.

You are good, O Lord, and your judgments also are true, for you give life to the dead and accept sinners into eternal communion with you.

Rightly you share your love, and with great faithfulness you guide us to your love.

My indignation consumes me when I forget that your love is your life.

Your promises have been tried to the uttermost, and therefore your servant loves your promises. They made an army of martyrs and saints.

Though I am of no importance and am even despised, I do not forget that you yourself were also rejected.

VI - No Limits for Your Love

Your goodness is ever flowing like a river, because your love has no limits.

I call you with your name, the name that you love. With my whole heart I cry out! Answer me, Lord; I want to be one with you.

I call to you; O save me from my thoughts that take me away from your presence. Before the break of morning I cry to you; I wait in hope for your presence.

Those who persecute me from malice draw near, for they are far from your cross and your love. I wish they may learn the power of forgiveness.

See my suffering and deliver me, for you do not forget that I am your brother.

Take up my cause, for it is in your flesh and blood and you have redeemed me by your incarnate life.

VII - You Save Us by Faith, Not by Knowledge

Salvation is you, Lord Jesus, it never was a doctrine; and thus if there is a failure of understanding, we are not abandoned as sinners.

Many are your mercies, Lord, that have saved and continue to save all who come to you.

Many are those who pursue and oppress me, but I do not turn because I have embraced your cross.

I am sickened with grief to see what is lacking in me, but your comfort revives me.

VIII - Give Me a Share in Your Love

See how I love your way of life and count myself as your disciple; give me, Lord, my share in your faithful love.

The sum of your life is truth and this truth is your love for humanity.

I rejoice over your word as one who finds that your word is the manifestation of your Person.

Falsehood I hate and abhor lest it capture me and turn me away from your Spirit.

All creation reminds me that you are not only the Creator but the Sustainer of all, thus I praise you because of your goodness.

Great is your peace O Lord; those who love you will never lose it.

My pleading you know, for you have had the same human life that I have.

My tongue shall sing so that I may enter into the joy of heaven and earth; that joy which you have and which you share with those who love you.

Lord, I have your cross in my heart. I eat your cross in the Eucharistic Bread. I sign myself with the sign of your blood, shed for the world, shed for my salvation.

Glory to you, most Holy Trinity.

Psalm 98

Jesus is the Wounded Love

Jesus, you made the cross on which you were hanged, your throne.
You sit on this throne until your redeeming
Love captures every heart.

The cross never was separated from you
Because you kept the wounds of the cross in your
Flesh after your resurrection,
Revealing them to Thomas to affirm your love
For all those who doubt.

O One who was wounded by love
And kept the wounds of your love in your hands and your feet
In your side and on your head,
All of these wounds remind you of us.

Grant me, wounded Jesus, that every wound of my life
May become a time to celebrate your forgiveness;
A call for healing.

Holy are you Jesus.
No one is like you in your love.

Psalm 99

Jesus – Our Crucified, Risen Shepherd

Praise you Lord,
King of love,
Good Shepherd who always seeks the lost sheep.
O what a great privilege to be in your flock, Lord!
For we do not need any extra care.
Forever you are the Good Shepherd
And forever you will seek us
In this life
And in the life to come.
In glory, you will teach us the secrets of the new life
Which we have but glimpsed in our earthly life.

Psalm 100

Jesus – the Hand of Peace

I have seen evil and it did not trouble me
For you have planted in my heart the courage to forgive.

Confirm me always in your love
To stretch my hand for peace, even to those who seek evil.
To wish them peace.

When the evil ones succeed in implementing their evil designs,
They may wake up one day
And discover that you have been waiting for them all the time
To come back to their senses.

In this way you trained me to walk with you, in your own way
And to live like you, carrying my cross,
Guided by your hand.

Psalm 101

Jesus – Tender Caring Wisdom

My God, my God – Jesus!
Help me when the storms of life are about to throw me off course.
My fear and my anxiety make me see my weakness
And my old wounds.

But you are dwelling in the fabric of my being
Almost like the dawn that is about to break.
You delay your help in order that I may learn patience.
Waiting is essential.
In waiting, you want me to defeat my despair.
When you shine, all that troubles me vanishes like a shadow
When the light of your face, O Lord, shines on me.

This false feeling that you are separated from me
Is hammered by the hammer of your incarnation,
Because your union with our humanity is eternal.

My body cannot be separated from me.
More powerful is the fact that you cannot be separated.
Even if my bones could leave me,
You will not leave me.
Blessed are you Lord,
Who unified my being with yours when you became human.
What a great mystery is your incarnate love.

Psalm 102

Jesus is My Dwelling Place

Bless the Lord, O my soul, for you have become his dwelling place.

You anointed me with the Spirit
And crowned me with the crown of adoption.
You counted me among your saints
And granted me the knowledge of your grace.
You established union with all of us
Exactly like your union with your humanity.

Blessed are you Lord,
Who brings life out of the dust
And waters the whole creation by the rain of your grace,
Who paints in the universe the signs of your presence.
The night tells us that you are invisible,
The day speaks to us about your presence.
The shadows declare the end of our time
And you anoint the grass of the field with your beauty
To call us to transcend that beauty into the eternal one.
Flowers and roses are the fragrance of the
Pledge of the imperishable life.
The trees shoot up high, as high as they can,
To transcend the dust which nourishes them.
Like those of us who transcend this earthly life,
So also may we become in our vision as mighty as the trees.
The sunrise preaches your resurrection.
The sunset sings the end of our time and the
Coming of the eternal rest.

Psalm 103

Jesus Can Not Be Divided

Lord Jesus Christ,

Your name and your person are only separated in a
Divided heart and mind.

A person without a name is made of our thoughts and
Our non-personal images.

A name without a person is our love for letters and the
Repetition of words.

When my heart cannot perceive the mystery of your presence,
It retreats to words and concepts.

O Lover of Man, lighten my heart with the fire of your love.
May your name and your person be the call of your love
And the love of that call to which we respond.

Amen.
Maranatha.

Psalm 104

Jesus, Our Creator, Transforms Death into Life

Lord Jesus, your power has been declared in your weakness. It is the power that accepted the weakness of the flesh, and death, and the darkness of the grave.

You accepted all of this, not because you knew it would end with glory, but in order to reveal to us that all weakness will consume itself. The limited body, the absence of life and death, and the darkness of the grave, are all closed circles. What is limited will come to an end, and will certainly die, and the lack of life which is death has nothing more to do but consume itself. The darkness of the grave does not possess anything, it is only darkness.

But you, my Jesus, accepted the limited and the finite, to open up the closed circuits of life by your infinite love for man, and to give life to what is enslaved to limitation. Your life is the life of the Creator who can create. You accepted the darkness of the grave because the light of life cannot shine except in darkness.

Glory be to you, for you are still in your power, working and dwelling in the weakness of all of your believers.

Psalm 105

Jesus – Love, Life, and Freedom in One

Jesus, you are the existence and the being.
I do not desire to have existence or being without you.
You are life, and I do not want a life in which
You are not at its heart.
I have no needs anymore.
You have killed my fear with your cross.
Death has become like one of my old dreams of a
Night that has passed away.

All my needs made me captive, in bondage to them.
But you, Lord Jesus, have freed me from my needs.
My love for freedom was not a chain,
For you freed this love.
Love does not seek a need
But is motivated by giving,
Not waiting to receive anything in return.
What a great revelation!
You became all my needs and all my wishes,
Thus I became free.
Your love freed me from possession, from fame, from titles
And from the desire to take.
All my needs and desires melted away in the fire of your love.
You became my only desire
In order that I may be united to you,
In the same way that your divinity
Is united to your humanity.

Psalm 106

Jesus – the Beauty of Divine Love

In the beginning, God saw that everything was beautiful.
Beauty became an aim in the plan of salvation

Your beauty, Lord Jesus, is in your conception and birth.
You united heaven and earth
By being born of the Holy Spirit and the virgin, Mary,
The divine beauty entered into our ugly world.
In our world, everything has its earthly origin.
Children have parents and their parents were
Children to their parents before them.
None of them ever had a divine birth.

But you came to be the divine incarnate,
To show us that there is a beauty in
Transcending the biological birth.
The beauty is not being dependent on biological laws;
The beauty of uniting divinity and humanity;
And the beauty of transporting the earthly into
Full communion with the divine

This beauty, Lord Jesus, became our own inheritance.
To enter into full communion with you,
Carrying our filth, our dirt, and our ugliness,
To receive the beauty of your love and the
Beauty of the divine birth,
Where acceptance is a constant movement of your coming to us,
Not only in your birth
But in uniting yourself as the head of the church.

O Beautiful Lover of Man,
May the beauty that is free from all biological laws
Be our beauty here in this life
And in the hereafter.

Psalm 107

Jesus – Endless Self-Giving

Lord Jesus,
Your life is a constant offering.
You are the bread that the Father gives to us.

It is strange that you take the name of something that we bake
After we collect the harvest and grind the wheat.
We make dough and bake it.
But you have reduced that whole operation into one word:
The bread that has been baked
In the oven of love
To be eaten by mortals.

We mutilated this great flood of Divine Love.

The big river coming down from the Father over centuries,
We divided into many creeks
In order that its power may be contained by us.

Lord Jesus, we even put you in a container called a liturgy.
Built altars for you and buildings we call churches.
We were afraid of the great river.

We even painted an icon of you on wood with beautiful colors
To escape from encountering your true icon,
Which is every human being.

Truly Love can multiply its work
But remains one undivided Love.
Only death can bring division,
But the Bread of Life was the medicine that was
Given to us to cure our mortality.

We eat that bread and make a theory out of it;

We drink your cup, not to love you or to love the others,
For we have even failed to love ourselves.
And when the seed of self-love is not in us,
We cannot exercise any form of love.

O Bread of Life,
May the power of the flood of your love
Remove all the obstacles that our egos have created,
That in you and by you we may have liberation from our shackles
And experience the power of your resurrection
And have a taste of the life to come.

Psalm 108

Jesus – Our Savior Before the Creation of the Cosmos

Sanctify me Lord Jesus Christ
With the sanctification that you had for me
Before the foundation of the world.
Create me according to the image, which you had seen
Before I was found in a body.
May the beauty of your divinity shine on me
So I become this image
Which you had seen and formed
Before I came to the body.
I extend the vision of my soul to see
How I was with you before I was created
And how I am now.
So that I may ask for my inheritance that you have chosen for me
Before the creation of the world.
In your person I have seen the Father,
And from you I have received the Holy Spirit.
You are the gift of the Father.
You who became the incarnation of the Triune love,
Grant me the eternal indwelling of your Holy Spirit
Who dwelled in you from eternity,
For he is one with you in the one Godhead.
He is the communion which you and the Father share,
That by having him, I may partake of the same gift of love
And enter into your Perichoresis
To be transferred from the slavery of nature
To the freedom of a person.
Being a person is the aim of your incarnation
For you have personalized our humanity in you
That we may become alive like you in the communion of love,
As persons moving freely
By the power of your love.

Psalm 109

Jesus, Your Kenosis Continues

O my only true love, Emmanuel,
You planted the tree of the cross.
I sit under its shadow
To refresh my soul.
I am never tired loving you;
I am tired, failing to be always with you

In the cup of the covenant of love
You poured your reviving blood.
It contains the fire of your love,
Burns all of the foliage, leaving only the gold.
What a wondrous joy!
Whenever I look for you,
I always encounter you hiding within me.
Once we drink just one drop,
We will never be the same.

Under the tree of your love,
I sit naked, where I have lost all forms of being.
To be is to see you as my life;
Not to be is not to see you.
Once I see you, I ought to be
Only with you and to exist only for you.

Narrow is the needle's eye of love.
It is only wide enough to permit one –
Two cannot pass to be one with you.
O Emmanuel, who came to us through the gate of death
To cross over our boundary of being
To live for us and in us.

The wise say Kenosis is terminated by ascension.
Did you return to glory in the empty heavens?

Have you ceased to be the Good Shepherd?
Your fellowship of love is eternal.
It will never end, even
When all the sheep are safe in the fold,
When every sin is washed,
And every stain is removed.

Human warriors kill,
But you are the one warrior
Whose love took him to death, death on a cross.
Whenever we meet you,
The marks of your cross say to us that
Your love is deeper than death.

My dark life became light,
My sorrows of the past became a song.
Your love is our new life.
In churches we gather to pray,
We sing to invoke your love.
When we preach your love, this is when we fail.

We cannot beg love.
We cannot buy it from the rich.
Blessed are the poor who just have love!
Under the cross,
I surrender to you
And there experience my first and last lesson.

Without love there is no doctrine.
The sacraments become mere children's games;
The Bible becomes just a holy book.
It is in the heart that you rest.
Pagans demanded your visibility
But what we see inwardly is pure.

The cross and the resurrection are
True events of the revelation of your love.
Love descends and rises to flourish even more,

But your incarnation sustains all of the
Vital powers that bring renewal.
By your cross you come,
By your resurrection you live for us.
Your incarnation makes us dwell together.

My ribs hide you - especially from me -
Lest I may become accustomed to you.
You contain me
So as to subsist with you.
This is the privilege of your love:
You contain me to give me life.
I live in you and you quench your thirst for me.
We exchange places for the joy of love.

Words are our medium,
But silence is the flame of love.
I speak to acquire silence.
In silence you speak.
How naive is it to examine your incarnation!
The two natures are mine:
One from creation,
The other by grace.

When I look into my face
I know that it is also yours.
You do not exchange faces
But form them of your features.

A king and a beggar,
Glorious and naked,
Mighty and weak.
You are more than we imagine.
You love what we call paradox
Because it is the sweetest part of love.
Without paradox union is impossible
And love is untrue.

Psalm 110

Jesus Has No Room for Ethnicity

My Lord Jesus, you are no longer the Savior of Israel only
But the Savior of all humans.
Truly you are the child of Abraham and David,
Born in Bethlehem in Judea, who came for your own people.
But you became yourself like the mustard seed.
Small and little, yet it becomes a great tree.
You crossed over the boundaries of your ethnic belonging.

When you died on the cross,
The humanity you took from Mary died.
It was buried in the grave.
When you rose up a new Adam,
You rose by the Holy Spirit.
Thus the Spirit completed your virginal birth.
Your humanity is no longer from Adam, but from the Spirit.
Alive by the Spirit
So that you became the mediator for all humans,
Not only the descendants of Abraham.

Blessed are you Lord!
Who have erased the boundaries of the old covenant by your
Death and resurrection.
And by your union with our humanity
You have established a new covenant, which has no boundaries.
You brought grace out from the circle of ethnic belonging
And poured grace to the whole of humanity.

Psalm 111

Jesus – Purity in our Filth

My Lord Jesus,
I saw your work in the new history of humanity,
Mingled in the history of the church
With our filth and dirt.

But I saw you crossing over all the boundaries and definitions
Which we had raised up against you.
Obstacles.
Ex-communications.
We gave them a dogmatic shape acceptable by us.

But you seek all, especially those who do not deny you.
Unite yourself to all who call upon your name,
The name of our salvation.

Psalm 112

Jesus – Compassion above Human Judgment

Lord Jesus, I have seen you on trial in our historical books.
So many accusations have been piled upon your head
Including abuses and curses.

We still have hundreds of Judases,
And millions of cowardly Peters,
And cowards like Mark, who left his only garment
And ran away naked at your arrest in the garden.

It is as if, in the plan of salvation,
You allowed all of these people to be around you
To paint a picture for us of how the gospel will be
In the future - how many churches will be led by Judas
And how, in our midst, leaders will arise who point fingers to
Sinners, asking them to leave the assembly
In spite of the fact that not one single person among us can say
"I have no sin, let me throw the first stone."

We have stoned all those who disagree with us,
Even about the interpretation of a word.
We hang on the crosses of excommunication
Those who were committed to something they believed to be right.
The whole of our history is embodied in the gospels.

The gospels were written to become a mirror
To see all of the stains that we have.
You did not pick up a stone to throw at the
Woman caught in adultery.
You did not curse one single sinner.
You did not even condemn Peter who denied you.

O you who are the compassion of the Father
Who overflows and fills the universe!

We dug canals and creeks for such great compassion,
Afraid that this flood of your care may carry us to you,
To be healed from our hatred

But you remain as you were yesterday
And what was written about you was for yesterday
And for today, and forever,
Not as a judgment but as an enlightenment
To those who can understand.

Psalm 113

Jesus Judges with Love

The Lord told me,
"Sit at my right hand, for I have lifted up all
Condemnation and judged you to have eternal life."

Jesus, you have not done this by the law, but by overflowing love.

In love there is no judgment, but glory.

I boast in your cross because it is the cry of freedom.
The freedom that comes out as a gift from you.

For you have made me the heir of your divine throne.

Sitting at your right hand, there is no law that will
Grant me your inheritance.

For what is yours is mine.

Glory be to you,
Lover of Man.

Psalm 114

Jesus Speaks through the Holy Spirit

I remember your words
And yet your words don't come from memory.
They come from your inner life.

United with us, your union with us
Is by the anointing of the Holy Spirit,
The source that gives vitality to our perception,
Gives birth to words which you have uttered
And to words that we will utter
Born of what you have uttered.

You are alive, my Jesus,
In the fabric of my being,
Hidden until you shine in my inner life
With an idea, or an image, or a feeling.

Awaken the sleeping hearts, not to worship you,
But to communicate with you,
To participate in the overflowing water of your love
Because you miss us and you long to hear our words.
The whispering of our hearts and the praise of our lips –
All of these are very precious to you.
You wait and watch the moment of our awakening
In order to illumine us by your divine light,
To become one with us.

Psalm 115

Jesus Unites Us by His Love, Not Our Achievement

In the assembly of the saints, I glorify you.
You gave me the boldness to be numbered with them.
Among the martyrs, confessors, prophets, and apostles,
No one is special in that assembly.
For we are not united by our distinction, but by our love.
Truly you became a kernel of wheat
That died in order to bring more wheat.

Your love did not permit you to be alone
But to spread your life to all.
And since then, all those who know you
Carry the sign of your healing,
Forgiveness, and the glory of your freedom.
Liberty from the slavery to sin.

O Lord Jesus,
With all these free humans I praise you.
You have liberated me.

Psalm 116

Jesus, in You Words and Actions Are the Same

I love your words,
Lord Jesus,
Because your words possess your life.
They come from your heart.

Our words carry not only the smell of our death
But the fingerprints of our incomplete existence.

Your words carry your fragrance.
The fingerprints of your being,
The truth of your person.

Your words are your person
Because you transmit your life to us
Through our letters, the vocabulary of our languages,
Because even in every language you became incarnate
In order to make all letters human.
A tool for our union with you.

Psalm 117

Jesus, Your Birth Has Honored Women

Hallelujah!
I praise you with your mother, Mary
My soul magnifies the Lord and my pleasure is in my Savior
Who became human for our sake, and took pity on our race.

Have pity on us, Lover of Man
Born of the virgin, to live our life.

Every human flesh calls you to be saved from darkness
And to shine by the light of your divinity.
Every human being who is born, is a call for you to visit
And to redeem.

My Savior, you have been born of a woman
But we still despise our women,
As if you came from the clouds of the sky.
But you entered our life from the vagina of a woman
To honor women by your incarnation.

We do not know how to honor women as we honor Mary.
We have not perceived your incarnation correctly,
Nor have we explored the depths of your love for humanity.

Nevertheless, you pursue us in every generation,
To awaken the sleepers among us,
To witness to the grace of your gospel,
And to praise you for the greatness of your love.

Psalm 118

Jesus is Our Freedom from the Chains of the Law

Many people have dug pits for me.
I have never dug a pit for others.
They desire to kill me,
Accuse me of blasphemy and heresy.
For you have desired that I should taste a drop of your rejection.
I did not know the suffering caused by the
Accusation that you are a blasphemer
Until I was accused that I am a blasphemer also.

When our lives mingled together, your being became my being
I look back and say, "How did I exist before I got to know you?"
I had the chains of the Law of Moses around my neck.
When you and I cut it together,
They accused me that I had trespassed the law.
Turned my back to faith,
Just as you were accused that you turned your
Face away from the faith of Israel.

My little story is repeated in every generation,
But the heart of all rejection is the eternal truth.
When love is absent,
The law becomes a sword for death.

Psalm 119

Jesus' Love Has No Equal

Lord Jesus Christ,
We define your love with our words
Derived from our visible, sensual life.
How can this be, when your love is so wonderful
That it is beyond our words?
It is revealed in flesh and blood.
Your divinity is the fire of this love,
Which we do not possess in our being.
Participation in your divinity is our only help
To transcend our mortal love to your infinite love.

Lord of Love,
Savior of Love,
Who came to save love itself from being subjected to the sensual,
To make the sensual transfigured by the glory of self-giving,
Which is not known to those who are prisoners of their bodies.
Our desires make us prisoners of our love
For we seek what is near to our senses.
After your resurrection, you breathed upon the apostles.
"Receive the Holy Spirit."
For by receiving the Holy Spirit from you
We enter into the realms of your love
To perceive the wonder of your self-giving
And how in every gift there is your being.
For the generosity of your giving is exactly eternal life.
Glory be to your eternal love which brought us from death to life.

Psalm 120

Jesus Did Not Live for Himself

You became a man like me possessing the same nature,
But you are unique in your humanity.
The center of your being is not the ego that separates
Nor is your life centered only on your human will.
But your human existence is an existence of
Union of the divine and human,
Which I am burning to have in me.
Your human will transcends you above all of our lusts
And your love was not from yourself to yourself,
But a divine human love that is poured in our human being
To make love for us both divine and human.
With your naked eyes you can see heaven and earth together;
Humans, angels, and even demons.
But our eyes cannot see except what we want to see.
Being a prisoner of our own being shuts down our vision.
You stretch your hands to feed five thousand;
We stretch our hand and hardly know how to
Divide one loaf of bread
Without keeping a large portion for ourselves.
You did not even eat with the five thousand,
But gave the food to the others.
Feeding the others is more important than feeding yourself.
That is what you said,
"My food is to do the will of my Father who sent me."
A human being you are, but unique in your humanity.
You are not stirred up by fear
Or by greatness, or by any other lust.
All of these are devices of death which are hidden in us.
You saw the prostitute caught, and your spirit must have wept.
And though you are without sin,
You did not lift up a stone to stone her.
For you did not come to give the law
The precedence of controlling relationship

But you came to reveal mercy for all sinners.
How did we manage to put the law around your neck
And make you one of the disciples of Moses?
We never understood that your incarnation is your total freedom,
The fruit of your infinite love.
According to the one nature you are my brother
And yet the word nature is so weak to express
That we are united together with the same love and life
Which you revealed in the uniqueness of your incarnation.
O Lord Jesus Christ, you are truly human
And what is more
In your humanity you have
Transcended what we know about humanity
And revealed to us what humanity will be.

Psalm 121

Jesus Inspires Maturity

You died for me
But you did not ask me to die for you.
You asked me only to carry my cross.
You know our weakness
Thus you asked us to carry the cross.
You did not tell us for how long or to what extent.
Your love does not know duties or obligations.
Your love was not and is not a fruit of your obedience to the Law,
But to the Father.
I can't compare my cross with your cross.
I did not die for the world,
Only to myself,
So that I may live for you.
To die for the whole world has puzzled me
Until I discovered the limits of my love.
To give up your life for all,
To abolish death,
Is so unusual and it cannot become an atonement theory.
How can your sacrificial love become a theory?
When in the days of my ignorance
I embraced some atonement theory,
I lost your overwhelming love.
Then you whispered, "My love is greater, for it gives
Life for my beloved."
O, my Lord, these were those whom you loved as your beloved.
All the sinners.
You still give your life for sinners in the Mystical Supper.
Once the spring starts to spurt,
It will stop only at the end of time.

Psalm 122

Jesus – the Altar Where We Meet

At your altar we meet
For you are always waiting.
You long to give us your life,
To restore and revive.
Logos Creator of our humanity, you have created us and
United yourself to us
So that your love may reach the human race.

You are longing to be one with all of us.
The more you create,
The more the circle of your love is extended.
At your altar you meet so many of us
Longing to be cured, healed and united
By your ever-flowing love where there is no boundary.

The gushing fountain of your mercy looks for our needs.
The more we defile our being,
The more the flame of your love blazes.
Not because it is dormant,
But because our sins are like a sickness that
Challenges a wise physician.
Our mortal love drives us to despair.
Your incarnate love defeated our mortality by planting hope.
Our hope is in your crucified and risen love and life.

Our mortality was defeated on the cross.
Give us your constant sustenance to live eternally.
The glorification of our humanity by your resurrection
Gives us your eternal communion and constant closeness.
O wonderful Savior,
Those who have a taste of your love will never go astray.

Psalm 123

Jesus – Supper of Love

You give me the Cup of your Love,
The same one that you drank
In the Upper Room,
To drink it with you.

O my Love,
There is no division in love.
Neither time nor space
Neither years nor a place
Can separate you from us.
Under the weight of mortality,
We divide.
Sin corrupts our perception;
It grafts in us
The importance of sizes and colors
And the material and the visible.

But love is invisible.
When love is uttered,
It loses its inner strength.
When love looks for the physical,
It limits its progress.
O my Love, the great invisible, who by your invisibility
Allow us to explore your depth.

Psalm 124

Jesus is a Healing Justice

When the waves of evil reach our necks,
We imagine that you are silent.
So we imagine that you are absent
Or that you don't care.
Some even say that you do not exist.

O, my Lord, what has happened to you?
When Herod chased you out of Judea,
Joseph and Mary took you to Egypt.
There you were a refugee.
How Pilate had the audacity to hang you on a cross.
There, on the cross, you quietly took the good thief to Paradise.
You slept in the darkness of the grave.

All of these events proclaim your presence, not your absence
Nor your lack of care.
For you were there to portray the design of salvation:
You meet our evil.
You appear to do very little about it.
You let it consume itself.
It burns its own plot.

Your love does not allow you to fight evil
Lest you became stained with evil.
Incarnate Lord, in your goodness you do not smash it.

A bruised reed you will not break, and a faintly burning wick
You will not snuff; until you faithfully bring forth justice.

Your justice is your healing justice.

Psalm 125

Jesus, in You We Discovered Our Humanity

Without your incarnation, I would have completely
Lost my humanity.

But your incarnation has brought me back to my
Awareness that I am human,
And my flesh is my visible humanity.

Without your incarnation,
Different ideologies and ideas would have
Carried me in every direction.
Even put my mind as a prisoner on the shelves of libraries.

I remember my body only when I am hungry or tired or ill.
But you Jesus, you were sincere in your attitude to your body,
The same one with which you were born,
And took with you to heaven after the cross and the resurrection.
The one you did not allow to rot
Or to be in the jaws of death.

Therefore, I escape from the universe of ideologies and ideas
To my real existence, to my body,
Which you love.
The same you took from Mary
And have glorified by uniting to your divine Person,
And now is sitting on the throne of your glory.
There I touch my own body to live the reality of your incarnation
That you have united me to be with you in the Godhead.

Psalm 126

Jesus, in You God Honored Us

My confidence in you is that you have become man like me.
A human who knew pain and joy,
Sadness and hope.
Life and death.

You raised your body and thus
Your body became an eternal sign
Of your eternal love for humanity.

Whenever I feel my body,
That feeling recalls your incarnate presence.
I rejoice in you because you are my life,
And the pleasure of my heart
Is your pleasure
Of being a human,
Living with us
A fully human life.

It is the last chapter of our universe
Concluded by your glorious appearance in the day of your glory
Where you will give your inheritance to us,
O Lover of Humanity.

Psalm 127

Jesus, in You We Discover God

I imagine that your incarnation is the
Truth that clashed with every imagination.
All my thoughts about the Father and the Spirit
Were purified by your incarnation, teaching, death,
And resurrection.

The teachings of the patriarchs and the
Prophets under the old covenant
Were the visions of our infancy.
They never knew you as human,
And so worshipped you as a Spirit without body.
But by your incarnation you revealed to us what is invisible.
Love is invisible.
But your incarnation, in your humility and
Life-giving death and resurrection,
Made it visible in the eternal union of the divine and the human.
So also power is invisible,
But by your incarnation, you made power serve.
Washed even the feet of the traitor Judas.
You had the power to drink the cup of death that we offered to you
In order that you might come back to us defeating death,
Even after we imagined we would get rid of you by crucifying you.

And although your presence is everywhere,
Your body became a sign of your presence with every human.
For you united your body with your divinity
And you became a spring of your incarnate divine life.
Your presence is not only a presence,
But a self-giving presence,
Transfigured at every altar in the universal church.

Glory be to you who, by your incarnation,
Gave us true knowledge of the Father,

Who sent you to us, incarnate.
You revealed him as a Lover of Mankind.
And when you accepted to be anointed by the Spirit in Jordan,
You made the Spirit dwell in humanity eternally.

You have purified and will purify all of our thoughts.
When we come to the furnace of your incarnate love,
All of our imagination about divine life will burn and become ashes
And the eternal truth will remain established –
That you truly are the Lover of Humanity.

Psalm 128

Jesus, Your Heart is Our Room in the Divine

We became your dwelling place,
O Holy Trinity,
Because you desired to dwell in us by the
Incarnation of the only Son
In order that we may dwell in you
And so that you become our eternal dwelling.

You did not build up a place for us by any created means.
But you built up a place by the Holy Spirit
When the Son came and became incarnate
And lived as human among us
So that the extent of your dwelling may be enlarged
To bring all humanity to become the
Camp of the Father and the Spirit.

Psalm 129

Jesus, Your Path is Life

O Lord Jesus,
Your narrow path,
The one you planned,
Extends from earth to heaven
But has its beginning in heaven
Because your descent from heaven
Made heaven eternally open for us.

On your narrow path, you planned to
Walk on this road by your cross.
On the left, a thief that had blasphemed and cursed you;
On the right, another thief who believed in you.
They are two signs to warn us
How the way of the cross is hard.
At the same time, they comfort those who are in tribulation
Who may be at the last leg of their journey
And can only shout,
"Remember me O Lord, when you come into your kingdom."

Remember me, O Lord, when I walk in the narrow path,
For the sea of desires looks clear and pure
But the dragon of death is hidden in its depths.
Remember me, O Lord, when I see deceptive desire as beauty
And imagine that I have life in it
And lose my awareness that you are my life.

As you said to the thief, "You shall be with me in Paradise."
Today and every day I am in your paradise,
Even in the state of crucifixion.
I shall go and knock on the door of the paradise
Where there are signs that point to the life that
You have planted for us.
The sanctuary, the altar, the crosses, and the beauty of the icons

All point to the narrow path.
And reflecting this kind of beauty,
Receiving a spark of your beauty from you,
I shall walk until the end of the journey, which is you.

Psalm 130

Jesus, Our Words Failed to Contain You

Many theories incite me to do research
And multiply my questions.
But the light of your love disperses my confusion.

Those who are ignorant of you,
They express their ignorance in the books they write.
I am surprised how they reject you
And make that rejection a kind of theology.
They want to rewrite your life
And even the witness of the four gospels are not enough,
Because the love of words and concepts
Has drowned them in self-seeking,
Which becomes a gospel that does not exist.
And none of them were an eye witness.

You were eternally before the four gospels were written
And they are only a witness to your life, death, and resurrection.
But your life, death, and resurrection are events that were
Witnessed and documented.
The documentation points to your life,
For we know life when we live it.

He who knows life does not fear death
And he who fears death dies every day.
But you Lord Jesus defeated death and its fear
And mingled your life with our life in order to make them united.
Our life together is not a theory,
For no theory has even one single atom of your love.
No words can express your divinity,
No words can deny your humanity.
They are too weak to contain any truth about you.

Psalm 131

Jesus – Gift of Life Manifested in and Outside Time

Your incarnation, Lord Jesus, converted the beginning to origin
And the end to purpose.

The goal is in the future.
However, the future is not what is coming, since you became man.
The future is no longer something we expect as unknown.
But you are the future,
You are the life that has no past.
Enjoyable because time does not play any part in it.

You crucified the old life
And the memory of the old life
And even the memory of our sins,
Which is the memory of the dead.
All of these have ceased to define our life.

But your remembrance is an existential thirst
Seeking this perfection which you have revealed in your person.
Your life is the eternal gift for us.

Psalm 132

Jesus is God's Way to Us

Jesus, you are the future,
The greatest plan that was given to us.
What a great alteration, that a Person becomes a plan
Where all ideas and concepts collapse,
Melting in the relationship and the communion.

Some of our ascetics saw you as a bridegroom of their souls and
Married you in the mystical marriage.
So our vision of the human body transcended into a higher vision
Since our mystical marriage was no longer a sensual union.
But by our union with you
We know that you explore the depths of our life
In order to plant true love in us.

Some of the martyrs saw you as a fighting soldier.
One who fights with sacrificial love.

Some of our teachers saw you as the theologian.
The teacher of eternal truth.

But all of these visions are about your Person with so many facets
Like a prism penetrated by divine light,
Giving us multiple colors.
Yet the prism remains one and the same.

Psalm 133

Jesus Releases Time from the Clutch of Death

Your incarnation made the beginning of my life
No longer a beginning, but an origin.
And it abolished the end by making my destiny a goal.

Future is not coming, but is always present
Because you even freed time from the clutch of death.
We are no longer ignorant of what is coming
Because it is you who are always with us and always coming.

Life without a past or a present, or even a future, is
Both interesting and enjoyable.
It is without a past because the past has been crucified;
It is without a present because you are the present.
You are also the future.
In you there are no longer the three dimensions of time,
But the eternal who is present.

You crucified the old life.
The remembering of the old life is a
Remembering of our sinful behavior.
Even our great achievements in the past
Cannot be compared with what you are doing with us now,
And the remembering of our sins is the
Remembering of what has perished,
What is no longer able to enslave us.

But remembering you, O Lord of Life, is a constant thirst for life.
A thirst for being fulfilled as a human,
With you, and in you.

Psalm 134

Jesus – the Foundation of Our Union

O Jesus you are the greatest plan that has ever been revealed,
And when a Person becomes a plan, all of our ideas
And concepts fall down,
Melting in the relationship.
As the ascetics married you in the mystical marriage,
Your incarnation has been elevated to inspire us.
Our union with you is a marriage
And even our marriage is no longer a biological union,
But a union by which we know
To dive down into our depth
To plant in us the seed of eternal love.

Psalm 135

Jesus, You Came to Share Your Being with Us

There was a time when I wanted to lose my being in your love,
But losing our being is against your love.
Instead you granted me, a mortal body, to be eternal
That our communion may also be eternal.
For you do not keep immortality to yourself alone,
But the immortality of the love that you have
You share with all your beloveds.
If love belongs to you alone, and does not overflow,
You would not have created us.
You would not have given us a heart that is thirsty
And cannot be quenched except by communion with you.

Existence does not belong to you alone.
Otherwise, why did you create us out of nothing
Except to distribute existence to all those who were
Created out of nothing?
To remain in existence in communion with your existence
And to confirm this, you came to us incarnate.
You remained in that flesh after your resurrection
Because spiritual invisible existence is not enough
To quench the flood of thirst that we have in our hearts.
For we will not have enough of you if you remain always invisible.
But you come to us, both visible and invisible
In order that the visible may be transfigured,
And our love may transcend what we see and touch.
Not to negate what we see and touch
But to take all of it with us into the ocean of your love,
Which cannot be seen by the eyes
Because what is seen by our biological eyes
Is certainly limited and defined.
But your love is undefined.

This is part of the story of your incarnation

Which became sour in Christology
And we have changed it into futile debate,
Left out the union of the visible and the invisible,
Which is the perfect revelation of divine love.

Psalm 136

Jesus is Divinity Shining in Poor and Sick Humanity

Today is the feast of your ascension,
Taking our body with you to the divine Shekinah.

We did not understand.

You do not want to appear except in the poor,
The sick, the prisoners,
The naked, the hungry,
And all the broken.
All of these are you.
Not because you are multiplied
But because your divinity became human.
And so your divine existence became in the image of every human
Who has a humanity that is shared with you
And, O my Lord,
That humanity is shared with you regardless of its quality.

The wonder of your incarnation is that it is
Above all of our mental concepts.
What an atrocity when we bring it down
From its glorious divine human manifestation
To our limited human language.

Psalm 137

Jesus – Love Given to the Unworthy

We say that you are sitting at the right hand of God the Father
Carrying in your flesh the wounds of the cross,
The wounds of love,
The seal of eternal love,
Which is a bond that reminds you of your death,
Of the nails and the thorns, and the spear in your side.
All of these are in your memory.
So when you remember all of this,
You put that remembrance in our hearts,
In the word and in the sacraments.
Not because you are a lover of suffering
Or have a joy in pain,
But because through pain you crossed the valley of death
And the wounds of the cross became springs of self-giving.

Your head has been crowned by the thorns of the earth
Those thorns that received the curse of the first Adam.
And the callused hands that were nailed to the wood of the cross
Will always remain open in giving for those who do not
Deserve your gift of love.
In every talk about worthiness,
There is a black cloud that tries to hide the light of your love.

Psalm 138

Jesus Receives the Anointing of the Spirit of the Father's Love

You were born of the virgin Mary and by the indwelling of the Holy Spirit.
That was the beginning of your human life,
A beginning by the two together, Mary and the Spirit.
In your adulthood, when you matured,
The Spirit who gave you your birth
Anointed you after you came out of the
Water to give you your spiritual birth
To reveal to us the beginning of your life as anointed by the Spirit
In order to become the beginning of all those
Who have a human life like you.

When the Spirit came upon you
The Father declared you the Only Begotten and Beloved.
The Spirit of his love dwelt on you,
So that is why you send the Spirit to us with tongues of fire –
Because our need of purification is so essential
That without the tongues of fire our love will die.

But the Spirit doesn't show himself anymore in tongues of fire.
He is too shy to reveal himself.
He enjoys working secretly in us.
If he reveals himself in tongues of fire, he will divide us
And show us who needs purification and who does not.
He did not come to divide, but to unite.
He is like you, Jesus, tender and firm, working within the Silence of divinity,
Softly singing the same melody of self-emptying.
He works without being seen as a hidden servant.
He sees our impurity and washes us by his personal holiness.
It is the same holiness that he takes from you.
He receives sacrificial love from your incarnate life.

Because of your incarnation, sacrificial love became
Human and divine,
Fulfilled by slaughtering the will and the body.
And by this sacrificial love the Spirit prepared the way for you
To receive that divine and human sacrificial love,
Because there is no human element in him
And the only human element that is united forever in him
Is in you Lord Jesus,
And the love for a sinful humanity is what the Spirit of
Holiness has received from you.
It is not just abstract love for sinners;
It is the love of Jesus that has
Crucified condemnation and abolished death.

O Spirit of Jesus, who created a flesh for Jesus
And by whom Jesus became a sacrifice,
Create me anew
That I may become a sacrifice like Jesus.
I ask for all impossible things
Because what is impossible, is possible
Only in the flood of the divine love.
And everything is possible for those
Who have the audacity to grasp it from the divine.

Psalm 139

Jesus Gives without Asking for a Response

O Jesus who has the saving name,
You love those who do not know you.
You do all the possible and impossible to
Make yourself known to them.
You communicate your life to those who do not know you fully.
You impose no condition on sharing your love and life with us.
Your love is unconditional and unlimited.
It is your person to call, visit, save, and liberate,
Yet your giving of your personal life is the greatest of these.

Psalm 140

Jesus, in You Love Became Participation

O Jesus, you alone are the teacher of truth –
The incarnate truth in your flesh and in your bones.
Your divinity is revealed not by giving us an idea about the Father,
Not even in a teaching,
But by reflecting in your person the person of the Father.
Save me as I try to work with this puzzle!
How can I, by ideas and words, become like you?

But you give life, and life transforms.
It enters through the gates of death and
Destroys our great obstacle – mortality.
And by giving us life, we get to know you, God Incarnate.
And in you we have seen the Father.
How does the earthly creature perceive divinity?
Is it by words or by songs? Never!
It is by participation in your life.
It is only by participation in the communion of
Love that we can receive knowledge.
Pure knowledge that has no earthly goals.

O Teacher of Love, you love us without reason,
But for a good purpose:
To give us a share in your eternal life.

Psalm 141

Jesus is Heavenly Life Grafted in Our Earthly Life

Your incarnation has cast out all the
Mythology that we have inherited about God.
For you never spoke about God, but about the Father
And your words were your flesh and blood.
You taught us the love of the Father by revelation.
With your revelation you gave us communion, and
In that communion our union with you is born.

Anything else is a mirage of the mind,
Sunk down deep into the stagnant lake of imagination,
Having a spring of death,
Feeding that lake with mythology
To run away into our imaginative immortality
Where the mind is constantly running.
Seeking life, running away from mortality
And because we have no life in us,
We sink down into the stagnation of our loss.

Until you shine with your life and call us,
Not by words, but by saying
"I am the life and the resurrection" is declared in "I am."
And so the ghosts of death flee
And the light of your presence casts out the myths of the mind.
And by the gift of eternal life you recreate our thinking
That we may become accustomed to think
Eternally in a heavenly way, therefore
Transforming our earthly thinking.

O our Life and our Resurrection,
The wonderful Jesus,
Graft us in your love that is overflowing,
Converting us from slaves to be free children.

Psalm 142

Jesus' Words and Actions Revealed One Life

O Jesus the Giver of Life,
You did not give us temporary gifts
Nor sanctify us by giving us earthly gifts.
For the whole earth was ours since we were created,
But heaven was not for us.
Death was standing and watching us, waiting for each one of us,
An invincible obstacle that we were unable to pass through.
But by your incarnation and crucifixion,
You destroyed that obstacle
And revealed the resurrection in your person.

When we separate your sayings from your life and your person,
We go back to our earthly life, which is guided by our thoughts.
Then again, when we perceive that your person is your teaching,
We return back to you because in you,
Life cannot be divided into words and actions.
And your gifts were not words, not even new ideas,
But the gift of life - your divine incarnate person.
In your divinity there is a spring of gifts!
In your humanity there is the revelation and
The sharing of these gifts.

Glory be to you,
The only one who cannot be divided into
Two after union with our humanity.

Psalm 143

Jesus is the Guarantee of the Communion of Love

Without love we stumble and cannot come to you.
We even made renouncing ourselves and
Carrying the cross like a law
To leave behind our past and to look for a new road
Without the crucifixion of our inclinations.
The self remains the center of our life.

But as we crucify ourselves,
A ray of your love penetrates our being,
Shining inside us to reveal to us all the excrement.

O Lord Jesus, by your light we see light
For darkness is not only the absence of light,
But also the absence of life.
And darkness cannot create light.
There is no light in us.
But when the ray of your love penetrates our being
And the cross becomes like a sharp sword
To cut off the cords of the false longing of the old life,
Your name becomes the song of our love
And the light of your way becomes clear.
For you become our birth, our anointing, our food, our life
And our inheritance.

Psalm 144

Jesus' Being is Truth, Not Ideas

You alone are the true teacher of truth,
For you are Truth Incarnate.
Truth is in your flesh, blood, and bones.
You did not teach us ideas,
But your divinity shines in your life.
The Fatherhood of God was not an idea,
But the revelation in actions.
We try by thinking and by words to be like you,
But you Jesus did not enter into life by words.
You have entered to us through death, to give us life.

And we have seen you victorious in the way you
Deal with us as the good Shepherd.
And by taking care of us,
We get to know that you are God Incarnate.
As we live your life, we get to know the Father,
And from you we receive the Spirit.
We perceive your divinity, though we are of earthly origin,
Not by words or concepts
But by participation in your life.
We learn that love is communion, eternal spring of true knowledge,
Which is born free from earthly goals.

O Teacher of Love, your love is without reason
But it has one goal:
The sharing of your eternal life.

Psalm 145

Jesus, Sharing Your Life is Your Goal

Woe to us when we repeat these songs using fast beats of music that do not give us time to think. We imagine that the best worship is to describe you, and we imagine it is an act of love, but this is a hidden disease in us, where self-expression becomes the goal of our worship.

To describe beauty and not to participate is like getting engaged and running away from marriage. To speak about who we love, about our beloved yet not to make him our life, is certainly false love.

We think that by praise we glorify you, as if you were someone poor waiting for our praise. We don't know that these songs do not allow our love for you to grow. It is like someone who saw a beautiful person, so unique, like no one else, and then composed the best description and the nicest poetry about her, but never tried even to kiss her hand, let alone to hug her. It is as if description is love, or a union can be founded on words.

O Lord Jesus, if you are in me, how can I describe you? I only can if you are external to me. But when you dwell in me and I taste the honey of your existence in me, I speak. Whoever speaks of the sweetness of the honey without having a taste of it is like someone who heard about a lion and praised his strength, but never saw a lion in his life, or even tried to catch one.

What a misery is our worship. The beads and the rosary and the repetition of words brings us back to our being, separates us from you, and this is how we deceive ourselves by worship. It is all because we did not start with love, nor are we looking for union.

Psalm 146

Jesus' Heart Beats with Ours

My heart beats and
Cries out, "Jesus you are my Lord,"
For you are the whole of existence.

By your sweet name,
My being, your being, and the universe are unified.

My existence becomes a song
Which unifies you and me and the whole universe.

It is a song of love, of eternal joy.
And when your love unifies me with you,
The cross and the crucified, the resurrection, the entire universe
Become one song, one union.

The cross and the crucified are no longer two ideas
But the power of self-giving.

Psalm 147

Jesus is Our True Life

In deep pain, I cry to you,
O Spring of Life.
We have learned from theology that you are distinct from us,
But our theology never taught us the mystery of your
Union with us.
When I remember your incarnation, my soul weeps.
I need that same union of your divinity and your humanity.
To be anointed by the Father with you,
To become a christ.
My deep longing is to be one with you
Even if that leads me to abandon everything,
Including my existence.
Because by you I have returned to true life,
For you are my true life.

Psalm 148

Jesus is Our Human Body in the Godhead

I have a body because you have a body.

By your incarnation, you have demolished everything false about God and humanity.

You made a place for us in the very Godhead.

Your incarnation led me to be a captive to your cross.
Your resurrection gave me life I never knew before.
What a wonderful life that you came to me before I came to you!
Your goodness has made me captive by the fact of the
Freedom of your self-giving.
Every beauty became a part of your beauty.
Every desire dissolved and became only one desire:
To seek you.
You became my freedom and my chains.
You became my love and my renunciation of what is not you.
You became my life and my death,
And when the spring of your love gushed with life,
Life without you became a burden, and even hell.

You are my birth, my death, my resurrection.
You are my dwelling place and my end.
There is no way to union with you except through death.
To die to myself, which is my desire to possess,
Is healing from the centrality of the ego.
And when I am crucified with you, you are enthroned in my heart.
Not to speak about your love, but to drink
Together from the same cup.
The cup that is your life
It permeates my being.
It chases out death with extreme compassion
According to your goodness.

Confirm life as a spark of fire
Purify all the earthly things that I received when I came to this life.

Psalm 149

Jesus – Our Human Awareness

By your incarnation you deliver us from our slavery to paganism.
Becoming human, you return our awareness back to our humanity.
The law of the old covenant is no longer a mediator
Because the law does not have the freedom of love.

But your love was too much for us to conceive,
And so we surrounded it with concepts in order to go back to our old illness, paganism.
But you refused to be defined.
Throughout 2000 years we still rotate and go around you,
From one idea to the next.
Imagining what you look like and what constitutes your real life.

But you escape all of this, because a defined love
Is a fallen human love.
Your power has abolished our death,
And raised our humanity from the grave.
Those who love you never return back to the shadows of paganism.

We have created many gods as our mediators between you and us
Because we have the disease of slavery,
Not knowing that in you, we are free
And that your humanity transformed us directly to the divine life
Which you have in you and share with us.

Your humanity has brought me back to the first circle of truth:
That I am human
And if I don't love my humanity,
I will never be able to love you.
But by loving you as human, I participate in your divinity also.
For you made your humanity the common circle that we share
In order that your divinity may penetrate the circle of our life
And that we may, eventually, become like you.

Psalm 150

Jesus – Our Freedom

O Lord Jesus, I praise you for becoming human.
There was no ritual attached to your incarnation.
You made the heart, and the tongue, and the body,
The realm where you like to be, and there is no ritual about that.

But we made you liturgical occasions once a year,
Celebrating your incarnation, death,
Resurrection and second coming.
So by our liturgical celebration, we put you
Outside of our humanity.
The incarnation is a shock to every ritual that is known,
Even when you were anointed after you came out of the water.
It was the Father directly who anointed you
Without the imposition of hands.

You are the negation of every ritual
Because if we follow your freedom, we will end with freedom.
But if we follow our rituals which constrain you
We lose even the free movement of the Spirit in our hearts.
So if we rebel against the rituals, there is a price to pay.
It might be to be hanged on a cross by the priests and the scribes
Or to be defamed by every worship committee.
For we, the slaves of systems, cannot live the freedom of the Spirit.

Psalm 151

In Jesus, Humanity is the Crown of Heaven and Earth

Everything you have created reflects your beauty.
And by it all, your name is praised.

Your beauty is in the colors that we see in the universe.
The variety of your beauty reveals the
Depth of your love for the visible.
And as you created all of these things to look
A certain way with our eyes,
You were waiting to become incarnate,
To see them as we see them.

The heartbeats of those who love you is the silent music
Which you hear through your invisible ear.
It supersedes the praise of the angels.

The tongue that is lit by the fire of the heart
Is better and more beautiful than the best candle
We can light in the church.

And the hands that can clap, rejoicing for receiving your presence
Are more glorious than the music of an organ.
For what is human is more precious than
Anything else in your creation.
You gave humanity that value by your incarnation.

Your presence in the flesh shines even after ascension
For you come in a mysterious way to our life
To teach us how to break the chains of our past,
That is, how to live a free life without the tyranny of fear.

I breathe the air that you must have been breathing
When you lived in the flesh,
And I can feel your breath is still in that air.

For this is how I understand my longing for you.

I love the water that washed your body when you were a baby
And quenched your thirst when you were an adult.
For you touched it once in order to extend your love
To what you had created.

You hushed the storm because you are the storm of compassion,
The storm that transforms our biological origin,
Planting us in your divinity and the
Divinity of the Father and the Spirit.

Everything has been unified by you
For you have not created the universe and
Humanity in order to sit and watch,
But to be enthroned in every creature
As a goal and as a movement toward union.

You came to us in order that we may live
And by you, we have offered to you water, wine, and bread –
Elements that you have loved, and used.
But you freed these elements from the circle of time
To make them symbols of your presence.

Psalm 152

Jesus, Loving You is Freedom

At times my heart deviates from being with you.
I don't know how this can happen.
But then I feel I am missing something.
It is my real existence, which is you.
Being a captive to myself, my customs of thinking and my habits,
I imagine that being alone is total freedom.

But I need to crucify myself in order to come to you.
I discover that we are playing a game of hide and seek.
I hide in myself so you seek me,
And you hide in yourself so I seek you.
But that strange game ends with the renewal of our union,
When I leave behind an old life and discover more about you.
You are so shy and you want to be grabbed by us.
Too shy, that is why you revealed your divinity in a human nature.
Not only to abolish our death and our
Condemnation and to bring us to eternal life,
But also to teach us that you are humble and
Shy in your approach to us.

You let go of me when I deviate
That I may drink the bitter cup of evil,
Then you laugh and smile
Because you have warned me.
But with the same smile you come
To give me the cup of life.
For you don't want to be standing, looking,
But you want to continue sharing our communion
By giving me your body and blood in the mystery.
As you told us, "Whoever eats me, shall live by me,"
And to be eaten is precisely the very visible, physical way
Of uniting you with our being.
For your flesh and blood is food

That nourishes us with new life
And in that mystery, you still play hide and seek with us.

You hide in the bread and in the wine
And we keep wondering, what are these two elements?
And you smile, to let us think that it is over.
We perceive according to the vision of our love,
But according to the vision of your love, we understand.
O Lord, let me drink the cup of your love with you
So the fire of your love may release me from the
Coldness of my mortal nature.

Psalm 153

Jesus is the Seal of Unbroken Divine-Human Love

My vow is the cross, the crown of your love,
Which you have been wearing since you became human.

The cross was not only when the
Jews and the Romans hanged you.
But when you emptied yourself,
You took the cross, the self-giving,
Into the depths of your being.

Your divinity shines through self-giving,
But in a human form in order that we,
In our little understanding,
May perceive such truth of love
Even as you have lived a long night of false love.

For you, Lord, are human without sin,
And this is something we cannot share with you.
But by crucifying your sinless humanity for sinners,
You reveal your self-giving to sinners, which is how you meet us.
It is your unconditional love that
Destroys all of our rationality about love.

In the darkness of hatred,
You shine with forgiveness;
In the darkness of the valley of death,
You walk with us to give us light.

When I make the sign of the cross,
Your birth, baptism, death, burial, and resurrection become true.
For the cross plunges me into the ocean of your infinite love.
I seal myself with this seal in order that I may remember
How to bind myself to you.
For my mind and my heart are

Rotating, changing, being a creature.
You are the beginning and you are the end.
And then I see, all starts with love and ends with love,
Which is your signature,
Lover of Humanity.

Psalm 154

Jesus is the Human Who Did Not Live for Himself

You love me.
You made your eternal dwelling in me and with me,
Not to protect me from evil,
But to make me a real human.
When I sin you do not take leave.
You assured all of us when you dined with prostitutes,
When you entered the house of Zacchaeus,
When you wanted the Samaritan to give you a drink;
On all of these occasions, it was you
Acting like the father in the parable
Who ran to embrace the prodigal.
And like the woman who lost a coin.

We condition your love
Because we are afraid to say that you have a
Special love for sinners.
O Lord of Love,
Love united the two natures.
But it is hard for us to understand such a union.
Our knowledge conditions our love.
Without union with you,
All of our prayers are puffs in the air.
Why and how do we call you, if you are inside us?
We call because we rotate, having no stability without you.
You are inside because you are distinct.
Our call is not to one who is outside us,
But to the life that we need to recollect.

In us and around us are the same.
These two words cannot change the reality which is above words.
In us is your longing to share our life,
Around us and with us is the immense care of your love.
When our words divide reality, this division creates misery;

When love transforms words,
This transformation establishes the continuation of unity.

Psalm 155

Jesus – Your Delight in Being with Us

Come Lord Jesus,
Rest your head in my heart.
You must be tired from seeking
All those who have gone astray.

My little heart is bigger than heaven itself.
Not in size.
But you have extended your divine presence to our hearts.
It is your resting place from the suffering of seeking us.

You dwell in all of us,
But such longing, we cannot express.
Higher than every feeling or emotion we know as humans.
It is the outpouring of your eternal love.

When you dwell in us,
Immortality comes with you.
The Holy Spirit sees you dwelling in our hearts
And comes to dwell with you and through you.
You are the mediator, the guarantee, the guarantor, and the spring.
All comes from you, and in you.
Because you yourself are the promises.
You are the life, the resurrection, and the eternal new covenant.
You are not a word, but the Logos Creator
Who grants perception to all.
To me.
So I can perceive your love.

You never abandon, even those who do not know you.
You remain in the heart of every rational creature.
But our thoughts and our feelings hide you from us
Because they try to define you.

You wait, Lover of Sinners,
To shine out with your constant divine presence.
You wait for a break in clouded minds,
In the clouds of our confused knowledge.

We cannot perceive your divine presence fully
Because our perception is divided.
We put our knowledge before our love,
And this is how we lost the way.
Our vision became blurred.

But you are the Light of our existence,
Shining in utter humility.
By humility we can receive the light of your love.
Those who have love can see you,
For love has a greater eye that sees what the
Rational side of the mind cannot see.
Love can also see what feelings cannot see
Because the mind and the feelings are
Chained by the weak perception
Which comes with words.

You have transfigured us from our biological physical existence
To true human existence.
Your love has its power, the greatness of your wisdom, and the
Beauty of your compassion.

You have shifted our existence from the physical biological one
To your eternal existence,
Which perceives, even in you, by bodily senses,
That there is a higher life than the biological one
When we are illuminated by the Spirit.

I say to you, "Come,"
But in reality you are in the state of pursuit all the time.
You are always looking for us.
But the call asking you to come is a call of a little baby
One whom loneliness has besieged and made him feel alone,

Which is the remains of mortality.

I am thirsty for life.
You are life.
Your name, Jesus, is the whole gospel.
When I utter it,
My soul
And my body
Enter into your life.

Psalm 156

Jesus, There is No Punishment in You

Unite your being with my being,
Even with the nails of the cross.
Unless I am with you, crucified,
The cross will remain an idea in my mind.
In a way like you experienced,
I have so many people who accuse me of things I have not done.
Crucified every day by their words
They revile me and they attack me without mercy.
This is the way you draw me to the circle of your suffering,
For the pain of the rejection of those who are around us
Goes deep into our heart and it wounds our souls and our bodies.
All these years since I became your disciple,
You have not reprimanded me for anything I have committed
Because you are the physician who came to heal the sick
As a physician who can see the wounds,
Both manifest and hidden.
And your love has no sense of despair.
You do not despise the wounded.

Your love drove you to meet the Samaritan woman,
To snatch her from her little hell of broken relationships.
You took the thief who was crucified with you
From the hell of his heart, to the paradise of yours
Because you cannot enter paradise alone,
Cannot enjoy being the only one there.

I have not received any punishment from you
For the new covenant has no punishment.
The first one had blessings and curses.
Even cities were destroyed under it.
But the new covenant is the covenant of the
Resurrection of the human race.

O Lord Jesus,
The disciples of Moses in the church
Imprison grace in the large cell of the law.
They strike, reject, hate, and even kill
Using the cross.
When they put the cross under the law,
They make God a creature, never a Creator.
And after they put you under the power of the law
They even ask you to obey their perishable theories.
And if you do not obey,
You yourself become the transgressor.
"Justice," they demand, "to abolish goodness, mercy, and love."

But you are not justice.
You are love that heals and justifies and raises up the fallen.
You are the holy one whose holiness is to reinstitute the fallen.
You enlighten those who are in darkness.

O Lord Jesus,
If you judge like the judges in our courts,
No one will ever be with you.
But you do not take your revenge on those you have created.
Why did you, good one, create them in the first place?
If you punish the weak and the fallen,
You destroy what you have created.
You become more demeaned than
An artist who destroys his own work.

But you have created us for your pleasure.
You will not rest until we are perfected in you,
Our eternal rest.

Psalm 157

Jesus, the Married and the Celibate Are Your Inheritance

I think very often of your mother, Lord Jesus.
The mother of all believers, as we say in most of our liturgies.
She gave birth through the Holy Spirit,
Yet our divided heart and mind
Has made that beautiful announcement a rotten soup.

Those who love marriage
Said she must have married after she gave birth to you.
And the Gnostics who hate the body and marriage
Say she never did.

So the icon of the spiritual birth
Has been tarnished
By our loss of innocence
And by our attitude to the body and marriage.

And if we ask you, Lord Jesus, to reveal her truth,
You will maintain your silence.
For you have taught us to use our inner eye to
See reality by the Holy Spirit.

Our external doctrinal formulas are not our best guide.
We still stumble in our divided perception.
We have not yet perceived the new existence,
Even of the body, where life comes from within,
Where you and the Spirit dwell.
There you renew our vision.
There you change not only our attitude, but also our life itself,
Planting in us the seed of the life to come,
Watering it by your kindness
So it may grow up,
And see that there are those who can stay unmarried.
For their life is not only in their bodies

But their bodies are in their spirit
Where you dwell with the Spirit
To revive and enlighten and guide the
Body into that new existence.
A new form of life.

We have too many among us who despise women,
While every male is a child of a female.
And so whoever despises a female, despises the church.
For the church is your bride, Lord Jesus.
And he who despises Mary,
Despises both marriage and celibacy.
Give us new perception
So that we can lift our heads above the sea of ink and paper
To see the reality of the new life
Which has been shining from you
And has given your mother this prominent place in our history.

Psalm 158

Jesus' Name is More Precious Than the Whole Earth

Food.
Sleeping.
These are not necessary to me.
Your name is more necessary than water, air, clothes, or medicine.
Only you, Jesus, are eternal.
All around me is perishable,
But your name is eternal and
Leads me to eternal life,
To the origin of my new eternal being,
The eternal being.
No one else can take your place.
Only you Jesus.
That I want and I have.
I don't care about covering or shelter.
I don't care about hunger,
Good reputation, or insults.
For any compliment wounds my ears
Before it wounds my heart.
In fact, being praised and being demeaned are identical.
You are the song of my life.
Whatever people can say about anything
Is a smoke that will vanish.
All that remains
On my tongue,
In my heart,
Is the song of your love.
Only you, Jesus.

Psalm 159

Jesus – A Lament for Misunderstanding Your Presence

O Lord,
What have we done with your supper?
We made it a memory, so as if to say
If we remember you, you are present.
And if we don't, you are absent.
Now what sort of love is that?

The Lord who gave his life for us
And was raised up to continue giving his life,
Has he become an idea in our memory?

Memory, O my Lord, is for those who are absent or far away.
But true love does not operate through the memory
Or even through history.
For in giving us your body,
You reminded us of the new reality.
Our body and your body are united in a new form of life.
This is not an idea in the mind.

Our giving is controlled by our thoughts,
By the value of the worthy and the unworthy,
By our lack of sacrificial love.
And that is why your supper became the
Greatest scandal in our history.

After you were born, lived, taught, and
Died on the cross, and raised from the grave,
You bequeathed your life in this supper
That we may learn eternal truth about love.
Love is not a word,
Not a hymn.
Love is a union,
A union of the one who is life with the mortal ones.

And when we are living this union,
It is not the memory that brings you into our life.
For you said, "Do this in remembrance of me,"
Because you are in us.
And when you are in us,
It is the spark of love that makes your supper
The celebration of that union.
Not of each one alone,
But of the gathering together the members of your body,
To become one with you
That your love may reach its goal
Where you are one with us forever.

Psalm 160

Jesus Gives a New Name

They called me George,
A name that belongs to my biological existence
And to the old creation you came to renew.
Society and my friends insist on using it,
Reminding me of my old created being.

But you call me "My son,"
Just like your Son.
It's a name that we share to point to one origin.
You even wanted me to share your throne with you
And to teach me a new language.
Beginning became an origin.
An end is no longer an end, but a destiny.
Division became the gift of union.
Body is a temple of the Spirit,
And blood is life.

But look, Lord, at the mess we have made.
We have imposed the old language and the
Old concepts on the new life,
Though you did warn us not to put the new wine
In the old wineskin
In order not to lose both.
But even deification,
Which is the good news of our new birth and our new growth,
Has become an academic topic for debates and contentions.

O Lord, you made me a son to your Father
In order to share that name with all of us who are
Included in that new relationship.
But we like the old names
Because our awareness has been educated to
Hang on the individuality

Rather than on the communality.
But our individuality in you means becoming a
Special member of your body
Who cannot live and function without the other members.
And still we have divided the body into
Better and beautiful and also ugly members.
We are afraid to speak about private parts,
So much so that we do not use their names
Because our bodies were shamed by the way.
We discovered them through guilt
And through the concepts society has put on us as a mental dress.
All this becomes our old identity and
Links us to languages, values, and customs
And even to our decaying doctrines,
Which were shaped by our old vocabulary.

But you, Lord, are the beginning of the new life.
The new that we have been unable to perceive
For the most horrible reason.
Our mortality hangs on the old,
That which is familiar to us;
And our new creation, which is a gift,
Is very hard to receive for a very simple reason:

We need to discover true love to receive it.

Psalm 161

Jesus is the Love above Academic Christology

Lord Jesus, I have to announce to you that
Academic Christology is dead.

But you are alive, risen,
Stirring up our minds and our hearts
To see you in a new way in every generation.
How often we like our old rotten ideas
Because our old creation is comfortable with familiarity.
We still ask how the divine and the human
Are united in one person.
We have accumulated too many volumes on the two natures,
But there is not one single volume on the one divine incarnate love.

We are afraid of your divinity,
Because it can change things in us;
We are afraid of our humanity,
Loaded with pain and guilt.
We do not want you to take it all and unite it to yourself.
We like to divide the divine and the human because that suits us,
Because the union of love is utterly unfamiliar to us.
Your new revelation has shaken our lazy minds,
And we are afraid to say that we do not understand it all.
So we classify your revelation in doctrines.
We treat those doctrines in the best rational way
And so exclude the mystical dimension.

But you, Lord – do you feel sorry for us?
You must have seen all of this before you even created the world.
And so you smile at us,
Trying by your smile to show us that there is a new way,
The way of love.
It does not deal with natures
Nor with persons either.

It starts with love without a reason,
The driving power of your incarnation.
But when it enters the arena of
Rational analysis and ignores love,
The core of the new revelation becomes
A debate of words and terms.

I am glad to announce to you the good news
That Christology is dead.
But you, Lord - you are alive!

Psalm 162

Jesus, No One is like You

O Lord, who is like you?
There is no one like you.
You became the apostle who preached to us the eternal good news.
Being faithful to the Father, you made us your
New house of the Father.
For your pleasure is to dwell in our humanity.
Such dwelling began by your Incarnation.
You made your glory shine on the mountain of transfiguration.
Now make your glory shine in your house,
Which is your body, the church.
Faithful Jesus, friend and redeemer,
We are your inheritance.
Our hearts delight in you, we are your inheritance.
We shall not be like the old people
Who never entered the Promised Land.
Strengthen our faith that our hearts may never be hardened.
For we will look at what you have revealed
To participate in the revelation of the divine love.

Psalm 163

Jesus is Our Sabbath of Rest

Jesus, you are our eternal Sabbath,
The one that starts and never ends.
There is no eternal rest, except in you, our true Sabbath.
Your incarnation is eternal.
Your incarnation became eternal by your resurrection,
Its ruling is the freedom of sacrificial love.
We rest in your righteousness from the labor of self-justification
Because through seeking to be ritually clean,
We have fallen into the sin of pride,
Yet you clean us by the Holy Spirit.
You Lord, the Giver of Life,
You chase away our mortality and graft us into your very life.

Jesus our compassionate High Priest,
Before you offered yourself on the cross,
You shared our birth.
The knife of the Law cut you on the eighth day.
You received the Holy Spirit on our behalf at your baptism.
You were tempted by the devil in every way,
Just as we are, yet without sin.
For you did not live for yourself.
O Holy One who alone is without sin.
You give us confidence to approach the throne of grace,
To receive mercy and find grace whenever we need help.

Psalm 164

Jesus – the New Boundaries of Our New Creation

Before the foundation of the world,
When there was no time,
The void was all yours.
Nothing can exist without you.
You draw out all the lines of our being.
You loved us before we even existed in this life.
You gave us an ability to accept you,
Like a seed waiting for the rain, to sprout and grow.
You gave us longing deeper than the ocean.

I came to being according to the boundaries of my nature.
To convert my nature to a person,
To change what is non-personal to personal,
To become a person,
I needed your cross and the power of your Holy Spirit
And your heavenly food.
I was forged in your baptism by your
Resurrection to finally become like you
This is the hypostasis of the becoming.

In the life to come,
We have a glimpse of your Kingdom.
Only enhypostatic life is the ultimate joy.
Enhypostasia has its roots in the submissive heart.
How is it possible for us to live as your image
Unless we become both hypostasis and share your enhypostasis?
Autonomy is never a hypostasis,
It is not a boundary for love and communion.
But love and communion are the foundation of life with you.

Enhypostatic life is rooted in your cross.
To die is to surrender,
To be buried is to wait for a source of life.

Then the dependence that your resurrected
Humanity has on your divinity
Becomes our entry into the new life.
We learn how to wait for the Divine Food.
To wait for your Spirit,
To wait and wait.
All is the enhypostatic life, which you rooted in us.
In Baptism, we receive your enhypostatic life by
The anointing of the Spirit.
Christos is not a name;
It is a conditioned life,
A life dependent on the Holy Spirit, enhypostatic life.
And so, we at certain times were called
'The Anointed' Christians.
Your second name was the name of your ministry,
Your dependence on the Spirit.
But we lost this vision and made the name Christ a personal name.
This is the fear of the enhypostatic life.
Fear to be called Christos is fear of a conditioned life.
Without an enhypostatic life we cannot love you,
Let alone our enemies.
Now tell me your secret.
I came to you as nature,
You come to me as a hypostasis.
I want your new nature, and
You want to give me your hypostasis.
I eat your flesh, which has both, your
Hypostasis and your enhypostatic life.
By receiving you, I condition your life by seeking me to what I am.
You condition my life, for you seek me where you are.
You depend on me to be a member of your body, the church.
Enhypostatic life prepares us for the kingdom.
Our dependence is that of love, it is not of nature.
Even the enhypostatic life becomes, in you, hypostatic.
In communion it grows up toward you
As your hypostatic life grows up toward us.

Then you come to my rescue –

Drops of wine and a piece of bread.
Are you in the totality of the economia of your salvation?
Here salvation and revelation are the same.
You have changed many things to hypostases.
This is the beginning of our restoration.
I eat you to possess your life,
I drink you to have your love.
You come to me when I call.
Before the foundation of the world,
You planned this mystery.
Without its eternal foundation in you,
All will be lost in time.
All will be swallowed by our death.

Your divinity is the foundation of this sacrifice.
It can meet death and devour it.
In your divinity, nothing can be absent, certainly not life.
So you take what is lacking in us,
What is not, and replace it with what is.
I wonder, and with me the whole creation,
How can non-being be filled with being?
How can death become life?
If the fullness of life can fill us,
We may imagine that all your gifts are untrue.

Blessed be the one who took off his glory to reveal his love.
Today is your day, our Lord and God.
It is the day that has no end, and
It has its beginning in your divine and eternal plan.
When you formed Adam,
You saw in Adam your future life on earth and the
Fulfillment of your love.

Psalm 165

Jesus – Forgiveness is Your Nature

Lord, I shudder when I hear preaching
That devours your love in the fire of judgment.
Our deeds judge us every day because
Our guilt stands facing us daily.
But you, Lord, the incarnation of the love of the Father,
The Creator–Redeemer, you do not create in order to destroy.
No, it is our fallen nature that leads us to such a pit.
We confess that in the flesh you were without sin
And still such truth does not allow us to see
Beyond our mortal vision.
For being without sin, you do not condemn sinners.
How can we say that you died for sinners
Only to destroy them later on?
I shudder, for forgiveness must be an eternal act.
But we made forgiveness subject
To our temperament and our vision
Which is marred by our sense of vengeance, and even hatred.
Restore us, Lord.

Psalm 166

Jesus – True Love that Unites

By your invisibility, you defined my boundaries.
You remain invisible to protect me from defining you
And from creating boundaries for you.
All the creatures are not you
Nor can they define you.
You protected me from defining you,
Lest I lose my boundaries
And lose you, too,
By my definitions.
When we recognize you through love,
We realize that you are Triune.
But if the mind perceives you through the Law
And numbers you by the visible,
It loses love and your triune life
And falls into a false monotheism.
True love that unites is true monotheism.
A monotheism without love
Is the image of man that has fallen from Divine Glory,
Transforming God into an idol.
Your love is always communion.
One God without love is a fallen human,
But only you God can live as love.
You reveal your love by creating
You perfect humanity also by creating us as a gift of your image.
Image is not an image unless it is in communion.
The image reflects your life, our Creator.
Like you, we create by words;
Like you, we seek communion.
Communion is only true in the triune life.
The Lover, the Beloved, and the Love exchange their life.
The Lover becomes Beloved, and the Love becomes Lover.
We know this in our dualistic love
When we are lovers and beloveds.

Our love is what we share.
But you, Father, Son, and Holy Spirit, in you love is a person,
Not a feeling.
It is not non-personal.
It is the person of the Holy Spirit.
For in you, person and nature are the same.

Psalm 167

Jesus – Our Freedom from Condemnation

You are the Image of the Father (Heb. 1:3; Co. 1:15).
How can we blaspheme you and say
That you paid a price for our sins?
If your Father is angry with sinners,
You, too, as his image must be angry.
You did not reveal anger, but mercy and love.
You are equal to the Father and yet you are different as a Person.

But you are in him and your love is one.
You share the same undivided love that has redeemed us.
Let your love shine in us, Lord Jesus,
That we may free our love from condemnation.

Psalm 168

Jesus – the Beginning and the End

Father you are the beginning of all.
In your love and mercy, be my end.
In the beginning was the Word.
Jesus, be the beginning of every word.
Lord, become the beginning of all my deeds and words.
The Word was turned toward God the Father in every act.
When you created us, you granted us a spark of
Your Word which remains in us.
We live, think, and act by our words - too many words.
But when, like your Word, we turn toward you,
All of our words become word.
A spark of your word,
The Word was God.
How beautiful that you are the Word Creator.
We are your earthly image.
We create out of what you have created
To complete the course of creation.

He was in the beginning with God, and
All things were made through him.
Without him, was not anything made, that was made.
Lost in the wonder of your divinity,
Each creature bears your fingerprint.
All belong to you.

Psalm 169

Jesus, Your Incarnation Was Not Words or Debates

O Son of God,
Who by your resurrection
Assured us of your love for our humanity,
Give us your life.
Train us in the school of your incarnation
To heal us from divisions and from the
Plight of theological controversies,
Which blind us and deprive us of the love of God your Father.

You came to redeem us from death, the old and hidden disease
Which is our desire to reach immortality without God.
It enslaves us more and more to the power of corruption and to sin.
These two, sin and death, are the twins who work together
And function together, one will bring the other.
But you, Lord, came to sever them,
And even to use each against the other.
You died that your death and your resurrection
May take away our self-seeking of immortality.
You became a sacrifice to plant sacrificial love in us,
And thus you have taken away the sting of sin.

Lord Jesus Christ, you came to destroy sin
By destroying its throne and that is death.
When the throne of sin was destroyed,
Sin became unable to pay us its wages
And lost its hidden power, the fear of death,
That enslaves us to all forms of evil
Even as we attempt to escape from our mortality
By seeking to create our own false immortality,
Which leads us to death.

Lord, you came to give us life, which is immortal,
But somehow this has become a matter of controversy

When our people ask us to give
An Orthodox account of our faith
In the One Incarnate Lord,
Our Savior Jesus Christ.

Psalm 170

Jesus, Your Incarnation is Beyond Our Use of Words

We speak of two natures in you, the One Lord.
The first that is from above, the second that is from below,
And is ours.
The Divine became Incarnate for our sake.
The human was deified in the school of
Divine love also for our sake
Without an alteration in its substance, its ousia,
To transform our mortality to immortality.

The Lord, whose nature is love, has united the two
And made them One Incarnate Person
Who is both divine and human, where love unites.
It maintains the distinction of the two, but makes them one.
One Incarnate Person in two natures.
Life in death.
Love dwelling in the nature that never knew love.
It was subjected to enmity and disobedience,
And sunk in its self-love,
So much so that sacrificing animals under the Old Covenant
Brought escape from the power of guilt,
But never cured sins.

You, Lord, did not say I have one or two natures.
Rather, "I am the life, I am the light, the way, and the truth, and no
One can come to the Father except through me."
We were forced by the rising of heresies to speak of the two natures
But we have to remember that our words
Are not the words of you Christ.
Lord, you are beyond our definitions.
Our definitions are signs, which point to truth.
But truth is not an idea, or groups of words.
It is you, Christ.
Because of your incarnation, all of our definitions

Do not contain the Truth
Because Truth became human,
To put an end to the good use
Or to the misuse
Of our words.

It is no longer our words, but your love, Lord.
The same love which you share with the
Father and the Holy Spirit.
The same love which dwells in your Person –
Not as an attribute,
But as life, as gift, and as power.
The unique relationship you have with the Father,
You came to open this closed relationship for us.

Psalm 171

Jesus, the Second Adam

What a comfort to know that you, Lord, had a human will
Because there is no nature without a will,
As there is no rational nature that has a real life without a will.
You, Lord, came to us to restore our lost humanity.

In your eternal hypostasis, you united yourself to our humanity
To enrich it with the goodness of the Godhead;
Divinity taking what belongs to us, and making it yours
So that a new order and a new Second Adam may have your life
In the divine union with the Father and the Holy Spirit.

Our first creation has failed.
But you, Lord Jesus, came to create a new creation
And to become the second Adam.
You have created in your person the humanity
That is no longer out of nothing,
But is a new creation by the Holy Spirit.
The first one stood between being and nothingness,
But new creation stands between being and eternal life.
Our first one was a being caught in death and
It fell under condemnation.
Our new creation is you.
You are its head and life.
Free, eternal, and no grave can contain your victorious life,
Our Second Adam.

Psalm 172

Jesus – in Worship, We Become Persons

I know that you are Three.
O my God, how different you are from us.
Different from us in your being,
Different from us in your love.
A community of Three are you,
While each one of us has made himself individual.
Even in a community, we are alone each by himself.
When we look at you, the mystery of your being becomes a puzzle.
We want you to be like us even in our sinful vision.
But if we make you like us, we will go back to paganism.
We will destroy our lives,
We will freeze to death.
Individuality is our idol.
Idols do not grow and those who worship them become like them.
Your mystery cannot be solved by our means.
Your life is infinite love where
Our words and feelings are inadequate.

Psalm 173

Jesus is Our Journey with God

In you, Father, Son, and Holy Spirit,
Three-ness is your distinction of being
And the revelation of the one undivided love.

You, Father, are the origin,
The divine beginning that is the source,
Beginning not in time or space.
There is no time in you, although you are present in every time.
There is no space in you, for you fill heaven and earth.

You, my Lord Jesus, are the one who
Brought down with you from the Father
Our new origin - the origin that was revealed in your flesh
To be the children of God.
Your incarnation is our journey with you;
The journey from slavery to freedom,
From mortality to life eternal,
To the glory of adoption and participation in the divine life.
Our divine-human mediator, you took us back
To the Father to rest with you in your origin.
You rest as Only-Begotten, we rest as begotten by grace
As your brothers and sisters.

O Spirit of holiness and utter humility,
How is it that you dwell in our sinful hearts?
This Gift of the Father was given through the Son.
You hide yourself in us.
You keep your hidden-ness to reveal the
Father and the Son-Incarnate.
Spirit of grace, you open the secret of the divine life for us.

The distinctions of your being have revealed
The multiple facets of your love,

Love that gives, and sacrifices, and dwells in sinners.
The Father gives us the Son,
The Son sacrifices his life to bring us to communion,
Removing all the obstacles that we have created.
And you, Heavenly King, the same dwells in us,
Taking from the Father and the Son, to giving to us in the same
Self-giving to make us one,
Which is the total mark of the divine love.

O I love you, Spirit of Truth, who straightens my crooked being
And renews it to be true to love.
While in us, distinction stirs up our fear.
Distinction is the movement of your love
Where lovers and beloveds exchange love.
But O, how hard it is for us to learn how a lover is to be a beloved!
The lover is a beloved and the beloved is a lover.
Thus communion is the flow of love.
The Two are easy to imagine,
But the Third has been above our imagination.
If two are in love, why is there a third?

O my God, the Triune God, how very different you are from us!
You, Spirit of Love, the Third, were called the Hypostasis of Love
Or the Third who receives the Love of the Two.
Hilary and Augustine and the great Richard of St. Victor
Have had this vision of the Third,
The Holy Spirit, the Communion of the Love of the Father
And the Son.
Thus the Mystery of the Oikonomia is revealed:
The Holy Spirit pours the Triune Love of the Three in us.
You the Third who are active and are dwelling in us,
You complete the circle of love.

One that is monad is a closed being;
Dyad can be the shared love of two;
But triad is a perfect communion of three.
Where the one is among two,
The two are not a number.

Numbers measure quantity.
The third is numbered to be counted for,
But counted for distinction.
The third who proceeds from the Father to rest in the Son
Is the very hypostatic love of the Father and his only Son.
And so, two distinct movements of love, Fatherhood and Sonship,
Are exalted in their Perichoresis where Love is made distinct,
But also is united.

Your Love, our Father, is distinct from the Love of the Son.
Distinction of the Hypostases possesses a distinction of love.
But the One Life, the very Being of the Three, is the life of love,
With no separation and no divided love.

Psalm 174

Jesus – Our Progress from Birth to Resurrection

Lord Jesus, you gift us by your life.
In the Mystical Supper you pour your life into our being.
Your love is so divine, given by the Holy Spirit.
O Spirit of Life and Giver of Life,
Life for us has a beginning and an end.
But you give us that which has no beginning and no end!

Jesus is the beginning of our new life.
He is also the end, the goal, of this new life.
Separation of beginning and end came with death,
But our new life is that of Jesus.
It began in Bethlehem
Where the biological beginning was from
Adam, to the birth of the Spirit
According to the plan of salvation.
Completed by the resurrection and ascension.

You, Lord, entered the heavenly realm
To give us our heavenly birth,
A change of our being travelling along
The movement from birth to the resurrection.

Psalm 175

Jesus, You Made Us Your Divine Image

O Lord Jesus, you did not keep the form of God to yourself.
You emptied yourself of this glory
To show us that you do not keep even your glory.
You are free from extreme self-love.
You accepted our form of a slave
To put an end to our slavery.
Thus you crucified this damaged form,
For you did not will to live for yourself.
By your self-emptying and by the cross,
You freed our enslaved divine image
From a self-centered life to a sacrificial life.
You restored to us this image by
Remaking us your image, to be like you.
In you and by your Spirit, we receive your new image.

Psalm 176

Jesus – Eternal Self-Emptying

Your self-emptying is an eternal act.
It is your eternal communion with our humanity,
Begun by taking our humanity from Mary by the Holy Spirit.

The Holy Spirit became a partner with your
Divine-human self-emptying,
And from you he has also taken a self-emptying
When he dwells in our defiled hearts.

Your union with our humanity is an eternal union
And it is the foundation of our being with you
And in you and in the Father.
What you have achieved in our humanity
Becomes our eternal communion,
The cause of our existence in the new life.
And when you come to dwell in us,
You continue your self-emptying because you shepherd our hearts.
You come to cure our hearts from ignorance,
And from being alienated from eternal life.
Eternal life is your very life,
The gift that you want to share with us.

Glory be to you who emptied yourself
In order that you may live with us and in us,
And that we may learn the eternal lesson of the
Grace of self-emptying that unites us with you,
Allowing us true communion,
Until we become one with you.

Psalm 177

Jesus, in You Division Became Distinction

For our sake you became man.
Through your humanity and this eternal union,
The eternal union became the reins that keep us together.

You are the frontier of the communion between us and the divine,
For you have brought all under one head,
Redeemed all, because you are their Creator.
What a wonderful provision, that each one of us
Has the same and equal portion, which is you.

By becoming incarnate, you made yourself a portion
Yet without being divided,
In order that the divided may be united,
And to bring those who had fallen into division
Into the eternal union.

For being God and man without a division,
You abolished all divisions
In order that our division may be transformed
Into the distinction that will allow us to rise up again to a new life
And become one with you.

Psalm 178

Jesus – Love and Self-Giving Revealed in Created Flesh

O Lord our Creator
Who created all visible things,
Making them the platform to reveal your invisibility,
You have taken our humanity in a special way –
To reveal in the limited existence of a human person
The invisibility and the power and the strength of your divinity.
But you have adjusted your divine Person
To the limitation of the flesh,
Revealed your love to the limited and the little.
And in the visibility of your flesh you revealed your
Love to prostitutes and tax collectors.
The kisses of the fallen woman covered your feet
And when she realized that this was improper behavior,
She wiped the kisses and tears with the hair of her head.
It was a very erotic action for you and for her.
But you accepted it, because you know
That prostitutes have also made their bodies
A platform of self-giving,
But in a wrong way and for an evil purpose.
Did you, Lord, learn from the prostitutes
That you, too, must give your body in the mystical supper?
They sell their bodies to eat,
But you give your body freely because of your fiery love.
It seeks our cold hearts
And does not rest until union takes place.
The mystery of your love,
If it is measured by our human behavior,
Would be a blasphemy.
But I wonder about your special love for the fallen
Because they have the audacity to sacrifice their being for
What they want to possess,
Even if it means selling their bodies to eat.
The method is good but the purpose is evil.

Lord, make me a lion like you.
Lead me to the den of your love.
For you, the Lion of Judah, do not enjoy the company of chickens.
Give me a share of the courage of your love
That I may love, without fear, the fallen and the broken.

When you died, there was not even a grave to bury you.
You were destitute, and even before that you were
Crucified with criminals.
Prior to your crucifixion, you ate with prostitutes and tax collectors.
You never showed hesitation to love the fallen and the rejected.
If this is not a sign of divinity, what else can it be?
You did not even cast out the one who denied you
Or reprimand those who ran away.
This is the Divine Love that is so strange
To our temperament and our perception.
So when we stumble about your divinity,
The way you showed your love is the best evidence for it.

Psalm 179

Jesus, You Choose Our Flesh and Blood to Reveal Yourself

O Jesus, you did not hand a book to us about love,
But you wrote (if this is the right verb)
By your blood,
By your sweat,
By the piercing of your hands,
By carrying the cross of our life,
The deep love that had been hidden from eternity in your person.
Now it manifests itself, even on your skin.
What had been hidden behind the curtain of eternity,
Now shines in the unity of your person,
Your deeds and your words.
For you alone are the one
Whose words and being are identical.
For such union of being of words and life is lacking in us.
You are whole
But we are divided.
Unify us with you
In order that we may become like you,
Such that our being and our words are the same.

Psalm 180

Jesus, Your Humanity is What We Need to Read

Because of your incarnation, Lord Jesus,
Our humanity became the book that we need to read.
Otherwise, you would remain an idea in the gospels
And the rest of the New Testament.

But you united yourself to our humanity
In order to reveal yourself in that humanity.
The book that we share with you,
Which you defined by your life, your teaching,
Death, resurrection, and ascension,
You have called us to read in ourselves,
Not in the words, but in deeds.
This union of words and deeds makes us
One book of one life and one love.

Without this love, you become like one
Who was documented 2,000 years ago.
But your humanity is with us and in us.
The humanity of the tax collector and the prostitute
That you refused to stone;
The legalism of the Pharisees and their hypocrisy;
The denial of Peter;
The betrayal of Judas;
The love of John;
And the unusual bond of love between you and the Marys.
It is the same story with different people.

Our great fall happened when the story became doctrine
And when the chapters of your life became historical records rather
Than the revelation of our humanity and your divinity,
Which you came to share with us
In order that we may redefine our humanity by yours,
And by so doing, we participate in your divinity.

O Lord Jesus Christ,
Deification, the gift of your love, is the road to freedom
Where we, as gods, live not by books or by doctrines
Or by the old records, but by our participation in your life.
This can make us free from chapters and verses.
Thank you for the freedom that makes me a god.

Psalm 181

Jesus – Our Humanity Is at the Center of Revelation

Jesus.
Witness (martyr).
Witness and martyrdom are the same in Semitic languages,
But the Anglo-Saxon tongue separated them.
Your witness is your life, not just your words.
And when you died between two thieves
In the place where criminals and enemies of the state are crucified,
You made that place a revelation of salvation
In order that your witness to the love of sinners
Will be historically true.
In the most horrible, disgusting place, where there is no glory
But rather skulls, and blood, and blasphemies.

Those who crucified you were standing by watching,
Waiting for you to die.
Thus Lord, Calvary became every human being
Who does not know you.
A thief and a murderer and a blasphemer are the places
Where you come to save.
Because you have been crucified on the cross
In order to be hanged until the end of history,
Wounded by our preaching and our prayers and our liturgies,
Which are directed to the good people,
Who are seeking to be good by their own efforts.

But when you died on the cross and were buried,
The light of the new life shone from the grave
And the cross remained imprinted in your body.
For since then, there is no love, no truth, and no salvation
Without nails and wounds imprinted in a new life.

Only a few of us will accept that contradiction,
To be caught between the old and new

And to walk, constantly wounded,
Until the light of the resurrection shines in us.

For we falsely teach that the new creation is created perfect
While the plan of our salvation, which is in your life,
Never was perfect by one action or by one
Segment of your life,
But rather by the totality,
Which we perceive only on the Day of Judgment.

Psalm 182

Jesus, Your Name Encompasses Our Being

You told us you call your sheep by their names,
A way of saying that you know each one of us personally.
But even in the old Psalm, you call the
Planets of heaven by their names.
The name, my Lord, is not an idea
Not even a symbol that we pronounce,
Or a sign that we have created for identification.
But a call that comes from the awareness
To plant the person in our life, deep in our heart.
For those who truly love, the first thing they ask is the name.
And to call the name is to call the presence of the other.
Someone wrote "I and Thou,"
But the "I" and "Thou" are the names.
The personal presence of each one of us in the depths of your heart.

My name in your heart is my person in you.
And when you call me by my name,
You have your own way of calling.
A longing.
A word.
A conflict.
A hug or a kiss from a friend.
To end the isolation, to open the heart
To the higher form of awareness.
Where in that awareness I can call you
And just say,
"Jesus."

Psalm 183

Jesus Avoided Self-Defense

I am with you in the wilderness.
I can cope with the hunger of my body
But the hunger of my soul is hard and a great burden.
However, by the hunger of the body and the hunger of the soul
When they are one,
I am deprived of my self-image,
The self-contained image that has turned me away from you.
In my hunger, I return back to you.

My heart is full of memories, dreams,
And the cacophony of a marketplace.
This disharmony has no link, no purpose.
It is this disjointedness that makes me enter
The wilderness of my life.
Feeble, weak, with the ghost of my old age hovering,
Making me hear from inside,
"If you are a son of God, why are you like this?"

How often I have wondered why the devil
Asked you about your own identity,
Especially when you were hungry.
For I know what hunger can do to the body
And I know what hunger can do to the soul.
In hunger, our autonomy comes to an end.

Our weakness brings us close to our mortality
But you refuse to change the stones into bread.
You refuse the triumph that will make your action
Prove your identity to the Deceiver.

But I have inherited from the first Adam
Those actions that constantly recreate my identity.
You have taken my error in order to convert it into a self-negation,

For error cannot be abolished except by a denial.
And the power of the denial was,
"I live by every word, not by bread alone"

Thus Lord, you have taken the two opposites of God and humanity
And in you the divinity was tempted to prove itself.
While being incarnate and living the weakness of that humanity,
You refused to prove anything.
For light does not require evidence,
Just like beauty
Has never needed to prove itself.

And so, you united divinity to humanity
In order to humanize the divinity, and divinize the humanity.
Yet in that process you never tried to prove yourself
Even to us who believe you and worship you.
You do not try to prove anything.
You let things happen
That we may freely embrace them.

Psalm 184

Jesus – Fire of Divinity within Flesh and Blood

For us you became human
And under the curtain of your flesh and blood,
The fire of your divinity is burning with life, with immortality,
And above all, with love.
You sanctified your flesh by this union,
Not momentary sanctification.
But it was and is a process, where it has to grow up in its union,
To complete maturity.
It did mature through the wilderness,
Through the garden of Gethsemane,
Through the crucifixion,
And through the darkness of the grave.
For in all of these events you deprived our humanity of autonomy
And planted in it submission and freedom from hatred.
You planted forgiveness and freedom from condemnation.
You planted reconciliation between your humanity
And the Father, thus ending our alienation from the Father.
In this, you established communion and participation
In the Divine Life.
And this, the new humanity that you want to share with us,
Is a process.
It will unify us with the mystery of your love.
We halt the process by words, definitions,
And sometimes by studying Christology.
But you are the dawn of our new creation
That came out of the grave
In order that under the curtain of flesh and blood,
We will rise up to the new life
Where all that is negative in us will be
Replaced by what is positive from you
Through the agony of Gethsemane and the nails of the cross.
Our cross is the force of destroying and rebuilding.
From the process of your renewal of the old

And giving birth to the new.
From abandoning what we know.
For the darkness of our knowledge is caused by our language
And by how our words and letters make us slaves
To what we think and speak.
But in your incarnation, you have abolished the language
And replaced it with a sense of life.
That is why, after your resurrection,
You told us that a sign of discipleship
Is to speak with a new tongue,
The tongue of love.
Silence means the process of renewal,
For words very often destroy the vision of truth.
Woe to us if we miss the fire of your divinity
That is hidden in our being under the curtain of flesh and blood.

Psalm 185

Jesus – Circle of the Communion of Love

You accepted my finite humanity,
But it never became a boundary for your work.
Instead, it drew the lines for our common humanity.
Where there is an intersection between you and us,
Where the circle of my humanity in you intersects
The circle of my humanity without you,
A new relationship has been forged.
In order that your goodness and your love for humanity
May be our common foundation.

The conception in the virginal womb
Is the narrowest finite form of existence.
And yet it became the womb that gives birth
To the life of the one who is the life of the whole cosmos.

You accepted our boundaries to have a taste of our weakness.
But you extended the boundaries by your goodness
To make those boundaries touch the glory of your divinity
So they became glorified by your immortality.

We were created out of nothing,
The border for our finite human life.
It was in the process of returning back to nothingness.
But you, Lord, have come to what had been created out of nothing
To make it created out of your life.
To give us a life that will transcend every limitation
Of our biological existence.

You removed the barricade of death
And you passed through it.

We, the dead ones, were sitting in the city of the dead
And in the shadow of its purposeless life.

But when you crossed over, you created an intersection
Between you and us
That what is in your circle of life may not only touch us,
But may flow from you to us.
That we may become truly your icon, shining with your life –
A life that the grave can no longer contain.

Psalm 186

Jesus, Your Love Made You Ignorant

O Lord,
When they asked you about the day and the hour
Of the end of our cosmos (Mark 13:32),
You said you do not know – you freely accepted our ignorance
Because love can close its eyes completely
And refuse to see anything, any day, any hour, any event.
For I believe very strongly, having tasted
Just a little sip of your love,
That you do not want to talk about the day or the hour,
Do not even want to see it.
Because you are the King of sinners
Who sees that in your kingdom some will not be admitted.
Those who reject your love, and that will be harsh and hard,
As if it is another crucifixion to you, a pain of rejection.
For if you were to condemn a sinner,
You would abandon your love.
For you, Lord, love comes before knowledge;
For us, knowledge comes before everything.
Because truly we have eaten from the tree
Of the knowledge of good and evil.
But you have taken love as a beginning for all of your actions
In order to transform the icon of the slave into a free child,
A transformation of that kind cannot take place
Except through love.
Love is the furnace that will burn off all the cheap metal
And keep the gold shining with the glory of the divine.
O Lord, our understanding of freedom comes from our nature,
Which is subjected to death.
For death has tied down our freedom
And made every choice in us harmonize with our egoism.
But you, in the flesh, reveal to us a new form of love
Where death was under your feet.
You even crucified death on the cross

When you gave your life freely,
Thus releasing the slaves
From exercising their freedom through fear
To exercising their freedom through love.
Truly Lord, I love you,
And I shall constantly ask you that I may love you without fear.
For even if I lose you, you will not lose me.
Because you have my humanity united to your divinity, forever.

Psalm 187

Jesus, the Sign of the Cross Is Your Seal

I seal my being in the name of the Father,
To return to my eternal origin.
In the name of the Son,
To explore my salvation.
In the name of the Holy Spirit,
To remain in the communion of the divine life.

This is the insignia of my being.

Psalm 188

Jesus, Our Hearts Are Your Resting Place

You made my heart your resting place where you dwell.
You come with joy and pleasure to clean
And adorn with your beauty.
Every time I think of you
It is not me thinking of you,
But the flame of love you have concealed within me
Seeking its origin,
Like a spark of fire that knows it will eventually die
If it does not return back to its source.
You made the memory like an ear
Waiting to hear a familiar call.
Thus my longing for you comes from you,
Like the air we inhale
And the air is all around us.
The illuminated inhale
Knowing that it is the Breath of Life.

Psalm 189

Jesus – Divine Love Revealed in Silence

Love does not need words or images.
These may act as a spark that lit the fire,
But in silence, all is revealed –
Not in the empty words of our hymns
Or the familiar and common vocabulary that we use.
Anthony the Great said, "The mind that created books
Can perceive without books."
And so also, love that has created the world and us
Does not need words for it is the pulse of life.
Thank you, my Lord and Savior,
From your love I learn freedom,
The freedom of love.
It is not about right and wrong,
But about union.
This has opened for me
The horizon of the divine-human life
Where you lead us all into the inner movement of love
Between you and the Father and the Spirit.
Take us with you to the goal
Of our being:
The Father,
The depths of our salvation,
Our union with you,
And the fire of communion in the Spirit.

Psalm 190

Jesus, Unfamiliar Light

In the synagogue in Capernaum,
You opened the scroll of Isaiah to tell us
That what the prophet had foretold is now fulfilled.

The release of the captive, the healing of the broken,
And the acceptable year of the divine favor.

For you have received the anointing of the Spirit to do all of these,
Not to pay a price, or even to forgive sins,
As we commonly use the word forgive.
But to release the captive,
For releasing is exactly what is meant by forgiving.
You keep no grudge against us
For you told us not to keep any grudge against each other,
And how often has our anger broken us,
Subjected us to brutality,
And made us slaves to our feelings.
But you have penetrated the depths of our hearts
To tell us that we have to see life in our death,
Not to see the death of others.
I have put on the garment of death from Adam without knowing.
I wasn't even there when he sinned.
In the same way, I wasn't there when you came
To invest me with the garment of life.
But now it has to be my choice.
To learn the royal-divine way of life, which is love,
That will allow me to be truly your disciple.
There, love comes before words,
And faith before formulas,
And union before doctrines.
All of these are not the familiar religious life that we have,
But are the waves of your light penetrating our dead time,
Defined by our inability to perceive without knowing

And to know what is unusual and unfamiliar.
For when we subject the unfamiliar to the familiar,
Which is the mystery to our usual way of thinking and perceiving,
We lose our true fellowship with you.

And so, we have consecrated days
Throughout the year for your life,
All of the feasts are folklore religious celebration.
O Lord, I wish that we had
Consecrated some days
For your teaching
On love,
On self-giving,
On humility,
And the value of sinners.
If we could have feasts for such teaching,
We would celebrate the feasts
Of your incarnation,
Of your death,
And of your resurrection differently.

Psalm 191

Jesus – the Unspeakable Depth of Self-Giving

O Lord Jesus,
Your love is for no reason,
And even the goal of your love is to share your existence with us,
And to help us discover this goal, gradually, as we mature.

But our fallen humanity has shaped our theology.
We choose in you what resonates with our needs.
From my broken heart I say "It is not different from adultery"
Where the attraction is located
In certain parts of the body of those we love,
And the differences are dismissed for the sake of our satisfaction.

But you, O Lord, let us abuse you,
For our feeble life and love do not defile you.
You walk with us and our defiled theology
In order that we may grow up and
Learn how to love without a reason,
How we come to you not even looking
For eternal life, but you alone.

Alas, I want to love like you, but my mortality deceives me.
I seek this doctrine, or that dogma, to fortify myself,
As if by thinking and accepting
What I believe to be correct and truth
You and I will be on good terms.
But you, Lord, look at even that and smile.
It is not what I think that makes you love me,
For you have seen me before the creation of the world.

Your love is above all of our perception
And yet in our mortal adulterous mind,
We like to make your love totally human,
Forgetting that it is the divine goodness and mercy

Revealed in humanity.
Glory to you, Love Incarnate,
For you have given us your glorious vision
Where everything has its fulfillment,
Not in what it seeks,
But in what it can share.

Psalm 192

Jesus – Our Covenant with God

The new covenant was announced by John's birth
From a barren woman.
This was to prepare us to accept the birth
Of the one who was born without marriage.
We are no longer children of the biological descent!

At the Jordan River, the Father expressed
His pleasure in you, his incarnate Son.
The angels had the same pleasure when they praised God
And shared their hymn with the shepherds.
The Father's pleasure has extended
The boundaries of our humanity to receive the Spirit,
The one who anointed the Only Begotten Incarnate
In order that we may be anointed in him, and by him.

O Divine Trinity, you revealed yourself at Jordan,
Not to enter a promised land,
But the eternal communion
Of the divine love of the Trinity.

O heavenly Father, I am utterly puzzled
For you called the one who put on the form of a slave,
"My Beloved Son,"
And confirmed that call by anointing him with the Spirit,
So that the form of the slave may know the freedom of a son.
For there is no enslavement in the Spirit.

Lord Jesus, by your birth from Mary,
We received our union with you.
By your anointing, we received the Spirit of adoption.
Your birth separated us from the first Adam,
And your anointing made us partakers of your anointing.
So, we were grafted into the Trinity.

O Flood of Love
Who would drown all our letters,
The tongue of the wise is silent
But the lips of the miserable speak,
And in their misery, reject grace.
In the chains of their enslavement,
They welcome the news of punishment and hell
More than the good news of grace.

But at Jordan, you – Father, Son, and Holy Spirit – you were
Pleased with the form of a slave.
It was even anointed, so that all slaves
Who share the same humanity with Jesus
May become aware of the transformation of this
Form into the glory of adoption.

It is the feast of your baptism, Lord Jesus,
That gave us our new identity.
We are the children of the free God who has pleasure in humanity,
Who out of the goodness of his mercy,
Never subjected us to any law
But poured out grace to the fallen humanity,
Calling us as his pleasure.

Psalm 193

Jesus, Your Love is Unfamiliar

"Today you shall be with me in Paradise,"
I shudder, I cry out loud.

Lord Jesus,
You went ahead of the thief,
To give him a place in your rest.
No confession of sins.
No time for repentance.
Love crosses every boundary,
Penetrates all obstacles.

Today I am with you in your Paradise,
The Paradise of freedom,
Where there are no methods,
No systems,
No dogmatic definitions.

Those who put on the mind of apophatic darkness
Can see the reality
That nothing on earth
Resembles this infinite love
And unknown mercy to humanity.

Psalm 194

Jesus, You Have Changed My Self-Knowledge

Jesus my Lord, your Lordship negates all that I know.

You have negated my slavery to systems and methods.
Those tools of our social obedience, are under your feet.

You have redeemed me from conformity to social values.
They demand giving up freedom and truth.

You have negated every form of slavery –
To words, to concepts, to analysis.
For all of these are our ashes,
But we think they are the best gold.

You have negated my biological origin,
I am no longer the child of Adam.
You have made me a child of God.

You have even negated death by your resurrection.
By uniting my humanity to your divinity.

Being my Lord, you have delivered me
From the tyranny of what the Church has imposed.
For you did not give us a form of worship.
You are the worship
Who has no frame,
No rubrics,
No steps, one leading to the other.

From the union of your divinity and humanity comes our union.
A generous, good offering, that unites us to your intimate love.
Confession "Jesus is Lord!" is the cry of my freedom,
The driving force that enables me to
Free myself from all that humans can create.

Psalm 195

Jesus – the Old Came to an End

"It is finished!"
And you gave up your spirit to the Father.

What a puzzle that we continue to tell ourselves,
That this enigmatic cry has multiple meanings.
In my agony, I cry out for the end of all agony
By saying with you, "It is finished."

In the completion of any hard task, I keep waiting for the moment
Just to say with you "It is finished."
And when a conflict ends with a consolation, it is truly finished.
When anger is replaced with compassion and forgiveness,
My heart cries with you "It is finished."
When I bury a friend in the earth
And look around the cemetery
And see the many seeds that have been planted,
All awaiting the day of the resurrection,
I know that there will be a time
When someone on my behalf will say, "It is finished."

When I am shaken by political events,
Torture and death and the destruction of life,
I have to cry out loud,
"Will this ever be finished?"
But on your day it will be finished.

O Lord, you have put an end to many things.
To the law, to merits, and to all values.
Yet death is still devouring many things and many persons.
Oh that I would be alive in the flesh to look at the end
Of my own mortality, and with the triumph of your resurrection
Say to death,
"You have finished."

Psalm 196

Jesus, in You There Is No Higher or Lower in the Bond of Divine Adoration

On the cross you bowed your head,
A gesture of adoration and self-surrender.
You adore all the sinners whom you came to free,
The prisoners who were swallowed by Hades.
To Hades itself, you bowed your head,
For the door of this dark realm is very low
And you must have knelt to enter it.
Like a storm from a little hole,
You shatter it.

Now whenever I see you on a cross without bowing your head,
I know it is my turn to bow my head to you
In adoration and in self-surrender.

It may be true that all of our thoughts come from our head
Which we need to submit to your love,
Because the fountain of your intellect bowed to me on the cross,
To help me to see the vision of your Father
Who has revealed you as his Son
In order that I may enter into that adoption relationship.

O Lord Jesus, may any cross, or the sign of the cross,
Become for both of us the rendezvous of the bowing of adoration
And our surrender to the immense love of the Father.

Psalm 197

Jesus Is Our Courage in Time of Death

Father, if it is at all possible, let that cup pass.
But let your will be, rather than my will.
To this cup you have called us,
We who are frightened, hesitant, double-minded,
Very unsure of walking in the valley of darkness.
For who can freely stretch his hand to hold the cup of death
And to drink it with total freedom?
Our martyrs gained this courage from you
But our mortality is the reason for all of our fears.
We carry the sense that there is an end for everything,
Which is but a vision of death.
The end of time,
The end of friendship,
The end of a good meal,
The end of pain and suffering,
The end even of joy and happiness.
It is the end that became an obstacle that engraved on us
Not only limits,
But the impossibility for a continuation.

Yet you, Lord, drank the cup in order that we may see
In your courage and in your submission,
A beginning, not an end.
To see how you are looking ahead
To your life that is not in the hands of those who crucify you.
You have drawn your being
From your eternal existence in the Father,
And now with that eternal being
You drink the cup of death
So that when you swallow it,
It loses its power over us.
You take what does not belong to you
In order that we may receive what does belong to you.

The exchange took place in your being
And in your cry with tears and a loud voice (Hebrews 5:7).
You called to our awareness
That deep powerful penetration of life into suffering.
Into Hades.
And into death.

Psalm 198

Jesus Came to Lift Us up to Divine Communion

O Love of the Father,
His only Son,
The one who is in the Father's bosom
Sharing what the Father is,
You come to us.
In us dwelling,
Never separated
From your humanity
Taken from the Virgin.
Our life is centered
On what we have.
What we want.
What others say
And think of us.
You Lord,
The center of your life
Is love that is shared,
And life that is love.
Your life is love
So holy that
It moves you to save
And make holy
Those defiled by sin.
Holy indeed you are.
In holiness you dwell in us,
Giving your life totally
In eternal communion.

Psalm 199

Jesus – Our New Freedom

O Jesus, my origin.
The old that you have created,
The new that you have re-created.
The old that was corrupted by me by society,
By our customs, by familiarity.
My being was captured by death, enslaved to sin.
All this was a catastrophe you could not bear.

The new origin from you, in you, continues to be by you.
O Lord of my life, I call to you
But you love silence.
You want me to understand myself,
On my own,
By my own means,
To see myself clearly.

Your love revealed you as redeemer.
You never were a tyrant.
You created what you knew would go wrong,
But you still loved that wrong being of mine
Knowing that I would yield to your love.
I started to love your silence,
To let me freely come to my senses.

In silence, your love overcomes my lazy heart and mind.

Psalm 200

Jesus – the Past, the Present, and the Future

O Lord Jesus,
When you were dipped in the water of Jordan,
You infused your holiness into that water.
And since then, the Holy Spirit has distributed your holiness
To all water in the universe.

You were washed by John the Baptist,
But you are immaculate, without blemish.
Yet you were washed, in order to transfer your holiness
To the human nature.
Come wash our inner being with the water of your supreme mercy
And wash us from the sadness of our past life,
From the burden of our life.
Transport for us your purity
So that we may hear with you, the same call of the Father:
"You are my beloved Son."
The pure call of the divine love.

O Jesus who was anointed for us and for our sake,
Transform the whole of our past.
For if we become captive to our past
We will lose our present, and also our future,
For it will become totally vague.

We remember the feast of your baptism
And remember how your love made you human.
Love which made you accept our humanity –
Plant this love in us
So that we who live under the hammer of the old memories
May receive the light of your love.
You can penetrate our darkness
And revive in us the seeds of the Logos
In order to shed all the superfluous definitions and concepts

Which time and society have added to us,
And which we have accepted,
To enlarge our being.

We carry the sins of other people in our memory
And we suffer by remembering them,
Especially those who have hurt us.

But Lord, nail the nails of your love in our being
That the old Adam may bleed to death
And the new one may be born.

This feast of your baptism is a call of your longing,
To be adopted by the Father, to become like you.
For through the longing of your love
And with your love alone,
We become free like you.

About the Author

George Bebawi was born in Cairo, Egypt in 1938. He studied theology, Bible, church history and more at the Coptic Orthodox Theological College and received his Bachelor's of Divinity in 1961. He was then awarded a scholarship and studied at Cambridge University, where he received his M.Lit. and PhD in 1970.

Dr. Bebawi taught theology, church history, patristic studies, and Islam at Orthodox, Evangelical, and Catholic seminaries in the Middle East, Europe, and the United States from 1970-1984. Through his devotion to church unity and ecumenical dialogue, he served on various committees of the World Council of Churches and the Secretariat for Christian Unity at the Vatican.

He returned to England in 1984 to lecture at various British universities and to teach at St. John's College at Nottingham University from 1985-2000. He then served as the Director of Studies at the Institute for Christian Orthodox Studies at Cambridge and lectured on Islam and Judaism at the Cambridge Federation of Theological Colleges from 2000-2002. He also served as the director of the project The Jewish Roots of Christian Worship as the Faculty of Divinity at the Centre for Advanced Religious and Theological Studies, Cambridge University.

Dr. Bebawi is internationally recognized as one of the world's leading scholars on Eastern Christianity. He retired from Cambridge University in 2004, moved to the Indianapolis, Indiana area, and was joined in marriage to May. He is the father of three young adult men and currently engages in public speaking and church ministry.

About the Publisher

Epiphany Publishing, LLC is a private publishing company based in Indianapolis, Indiana. We are devoted to exploring and socializing catalysts for growth in the fields of religion, psychology, business, and human development.

Each year, Epiphany Publishing donates at least 25 percent of all its profits to nonprofit organizations that fight profound injustice—especially those atrocities that rob the innocent of their future. This includes the global sex trade, child soldiers forced to fight in war, and other forms of unthinkable oppression. We invite you to join us in partnering with luminous, restorative organizations like saribari.com, warchild.org, worldvision.org, and antislavery.org.

We are always interested in meeting new authors and reviewing promising manuscripts. If you've got a transformational message that you believe would be a good fit to publish with us, please introduce yourself at epiphanypublishing.us.

Made in the USA
Monee, IL
08 March 2020

22922259R00173